EXPERIENCES OF
COUNSELLING
IN

**COUNSELLING
· IN ACTION ·**

Series editor: Windy Dryden

Counselling in Action is a series of books developed
especially for counsellors and students of
counselling which provides clear and explicit
guidelines for counselling practice. A special feature
of the series is the emphasis it places on the *process*
of counselling.

Feminist Counselling in Action
Jocelyn Chaplin

Gestalt Counselling in Action
Petrūska Clarkson

Transcultural Counselling in Action
Patricia d'Ardenne and Aruna Mahtani

Key Issues for Counselling in Action
edited by Windy Dryden

Rational-Emotive Counselling in Action
Windy Dryden

Psychodynamic Counselling in Action
Michael Jacobs

Experiences of Counselling in Action
edited by Dave Mearns and Windy Dryden

Person-Centred Counselling in Action
Dave Mearns and Brian Thorne

Transactional Analysis Counselling in Action
Ian Stewart

Cognitive-Behavioural Counselling in Action
Peter Trower, Andrew Casey and Windy Dryden

EXPERIENCES OF COUNSELLING
IN *Action*

edited by
DAVE MEARNS and WINDY DRYDEN

SAGE Publications
London • Thousand Oaks • New Delhi

© Dave Means and Windy Dryden 1990

First published 1990
Reprinted 1990, 1993, 1994, 1998, 2000

SAGE Publications Ltd
6 Bonhill Street
London EC2A 4PU

SAGE Publications Inc
2455 Teller Road
Thousand Oaks, California 91320

SAGE Publications India Pvt Ltd
32, M-Block Market
Greater Kailash – I
New Delhi 110 048

British Library Cataloguing in Publication Data

Experiences of counselling in action – (Counselling
  in action).
  1. Counselling
  I. Mearns, Dave   II. Dryden, Windy   III. Series
  361.3′23

ISBN 0-8039-8192-9
ISBN 0-8039-8193-7 Pbk

Library of Congress catalog card number 89–063698

Typeset by Photoprint, Torquay, Devon
Printed in Great Britain by
Redwood Books , Trowbridge, Wiltshire

Contents

Preface

Counselling is one of the more intense human experiences for both client and counsellor. For the client, the counselling hour may represent an oasis of meaningful communication amidst a life filled with manipulative relationships, unexpressed feelings and a sense of hopelessness. Counselling can also be a frightening experience with the client finding himself coming face to face with difficulties he has pushed aside for many years. Clients' experiences in counselling are as varied as the clients themselves, but the *intensity* of the experience tends to be a common feature — as a client of one of the editors said: 'Counselling is like living with your finger on the "fast-forward" button — you can go through an enormous amount of living in just one hour.'

The experience for the counsellor is different but it too carries an intensity and immediacy which is matched by few professions. The counsellor, regardless of her specific counselling approach, is being a 'supportive challenger' to the client. She is working in the midst of the client's thoughts and feelings, trying to retain her coherence even though those thoughts and feelings seem hopelessly confused and desperate. As one counsellor involved in the investigations for this book said, 'The difference between counselling and "real life" is that you have to be more "alive" in counselling.' Added to these feelings in the client and counsellor is the whole unpredictability of the experience. The client rarely knows what is going to happen in the next hour and the counsellor never knows. This intensity and unpredictability of the counselling experience may in part explain its attraction for both client and counsellor.

This book samples counselling in action as it is experienced by both clients and counsellors. Apart from the chapters on research literature, all the authors were asked to write as personally as possible about their experiences of different aspects of counselling. The first half of the book is devoted to the experiences of clients and begins with John McLeod's review of the research literature, including the fascinating recent work by Rennie (1984, 1985a, 1985b and 1987).

Chapter 2 is the shortest in the book, yet the editors will not be surprised if it is the chapter that many readers find to be most evocative. In this chapter Laura Allen provides a unique account of the experience of failure in counselling from the client's perspective.

Laura describes two experiences which failed for quite different reasons. In the first her experience was of being abused and in the second it was of working with an ineffectual counsellor. The power of Laura's writing comes in part from the fact that she is able to analyse these failed experiences in a critical way which is disturbingly convincing for practitioners as well as other clients.

In Chapter 3, Myra Grierson addresses the experience of success as a client. She also describes two quite different counselling experiences which were both important to her at different times in her life. The first 'kept her alive' while the second helped her to tackle conflicts left over from childhood. In both cases Myra gives an enlightening account of how she found her own 'power' in the context of these relationships with her counsellors.

Writing about the experience of couple counselling carries the added complication of trying to reflect the experiences of both partners. Rosanne and Paul accomplish this by agreeing on many parts of the experience in Chapter 4 but also representing their own individual reactions to the same events.

Chapter 5 represents a bridging chapter from the client's experience to the counsellor's experience in that its author, Brendan McLoughlin, had two experiences as a client on his way to becoming a counsellor and psychotherapist. Our request of Brendan was that he should examine how these experiences of being a client influenced him in his later work as a counsellor. It is quite common in counselling and psychotherapy training to invite the trainee to be a client — in fact on some training courses it is seen as essential that the trainee has experience in the 'other seat'. Brendan's chapter gives some personal insights into why this should be important.

The second half of the book is devoted to the experiences of counsellors. In Chapter 6 John McLeod reviews the research literature on the counsellor's experience and includes a challenge to researchers and practitioners to explore the effects of communication at different levels in the counselling relationship. For instance, just as important as the counsellor's experience of the client is the counsellor's assumptions about how the client experiences her!

Dave Mearns uses Chapters 7 and 8 to explore counsellors' experiences of 'failure' and 'success'. Rather than give one practitioner's account of failure and success, Dave investigated the experiences of sixty-one practitioners on the issue of failure and forty-eight on success. These chapters explore how counsellors construe 'failure' and 'success' and give personal accounts of how they have experienced events such as a client's sudden discontinuation and indeed a client's suicide, as well as the more 'successful' endeavours of counsellors such as employing flexible working practices.

In Chapter 9, Senga Blackie illustrates her experience as a counsellor through her work with two couples, the first for a brief three sessions and the second as a long-term commitment which saw her work first with the woman, then the couple and finally both partners separately. In this chapter Senga shows how her approach to work with couples is to regard the relationship between the partners as an entity in itself to which she must relate in the same way as with the individuals.

In Chapter 10 the editors examine the kind of issues which recur in these experiences of clients and counsellors throughout the book and coin the term 'the unspoken relationship' to denote those aspects of the relationship between client and counsellor which are experienced by each but rarely addressed.

The counselling approaches reflected in this book include Gestalt, Transactional Analysis and other humanistic approaches to counselling. However, the vast majority of client and counsellor experiences come from the person-centred and psychodynamic traditions. This is especially the case in Chapters 7 and 8 where Dave Mearns reviews the experiences of large numbers of practitioners. An interesting observation from results of that survey is that the differences in counselling approach were much less evident in the descriptions given by more experienced practitioners. This finding reflects those of earlier researchers such as Fiedler (1950) and Raskin (1974). Sharper contrasts among experiences of counselling might have been evident if this book had adequately canvassed the views of cognitive-behavioural workers, but this approach more than any other is underrepresented in the present text as it is in the field of counselling in Britain.

In writing in this domain there is a perennial problem concerning the appropriateness of the terms 'counselling' and 'therapy'. Sometimes it is felt that work which goes on for a lengthy period of, say, a year or more should properly be called 'therapy' rather than 'counselling'. Yet the actual duration does not necessarily imply a difference in the processes or functions of the work, so this basis for distinguishing between them is rather weak. Sometimes workers will use the word 'therapy' when the issues the client is endeavouring to tackle are particularly deep seated, reaching back into expectations and patterns created in childhood, whereas 'counselling' might be used to refer to work on more transient problems such as may arise from changes occurring in the client's life or crises in relationships. However, this distinction is not as neat as it looks because a major part of the difficulty with changes or crises is that dealing with them will usually involve the client becoming aware of deep-seated expectations, patterns of relating and conflicts from earlier life which should properly be worked with by the practitioner whether she regards herself as a 'counsellor' or 'therapist'. The question of the difference between these labels becomes even more spurious when we examine cultural differences — for instance, much that is called counselling in Britain would be therapy in the United States of America! Furthermore, the major traditions differ in their terminologies. The person-centred approach, for instance, deliberately does not distinguish between the terms on the grounds that the interpersonal processes are the same, whereas the psycho-dynamic tradition does offer a distinction in which dealing with the transference relationship is much more central to psychodynamic *therapy*.

Since this series of books uses the term 'counselling' we have also followed that convention in most instances. An obvious exception to that is in the chapters on the research literature where the researchers themselves, often American, would tend to use the term 'therapy'. Most of our chapter authors have referred to their work as 'counselling' although it must be said that a few of them would more often use the word 'therapy' to describe their work, particularly those with a strong psychodynamic influence like Brendan McLoughlin, and Paul and Rosanne, for whom the term 'therapy' would have been preferred on the grounds that their experience involved considerable work with unconscious material. Really, the question of whether the term 'counselling' or 'therapy' is the more appropriate term is not of crucial significance — indeed, clients sometimes devise other names for their practitioners like 'my consultant' or 'my facilitator'. Much more interesting and important than terminology are questions like: 'How does the counsellor *experience* what is going on?' and 'What is the client's *experience*?' It is these questions that the present volume seeks to explore.

Dave Mearns, Glasgow
Windy Dryden, London

1 The Client's Experience of Counselling and Psychotherapy: A Review of the Research Literature

John McLeod

'How did the client view the objectives of our work together? I don't really know. . . . You *keep* asking me this question and it makes me think. . . .'
'I often wish I knew what my clients think of me . . . maybe I should ask them!' (Quotations from interviews with therapists conducted by Maluccio, 1979.)

Hardly anyone has ever asked clients what they think about the counselling or psychotherapy they are receiving. The longest chapter in *Client-Centered Therapy*, published in 1951, is an attempt by Carl Rogers to examine 'the therapeutic relationship as experienced by the client'. At the end of that chapter Rogers (1951: 130) comments on 'how little this whole field has been explored'. The following decades have not, however, witnessed much more than a handful of further exploratory journeys into this particular territory. Rennie (1985a: 2), as one of the most recent of these explorers, commented that 'in the history of research in psychotherapy . . . direct inquiry into the client's experience has seldom been undertaken'. In this chapter, the few studies which have been undertaken into the client's experience of counselling will be reviewed. Before turning to that task, however, it is worth reflecting on the possible reasons for the absence of research studies in this area. Why have researchers shown so little interest in the ways that clients make sense of their involvement in counselling or psychotherapy? Why is it so difficult to find the voice of the consumer in the literature in this field?

There is no simple reason for this neglect: the absence of research into the client's experience of counselling or psychotherapy needs to be understood as resulting from the convergence of a number of powerful forces at work within the profession as a whole. There are for example strong institutional pressures on people who carry out research to follow the assumptions and practices of natural science

— in other words to make reliable, objective measurements of variables derived from theories or models, and to exert some sort of experimental control over the phenomena being studied, in order to test hypotheses. From this perspective, the subjective feelings, states of mind or beliefs of clients are not legitimate topics of interest — they are just not researchable. Another significant factor in the neglect of the client's experience has been the influence of psychoanalytic theory on both researchers and practitioners. From a psychoanalytic point of view, what the client says about his or her experience will often be interpreted as evidence of defensiveness, fantasy or transference. It is therefore difficult for psychoanalytically oriented writers to take clients' accounts of their experiences at face value. Further, even though their theoretical model is very different, behavioural theorists and researchers are similarly sceptical about the usefulness of what clients have to say about their experience. For behaviourists, it has traditionally been more important to focus on client *behaviour* and how it can be changed, than to be concerned with vague internal events such as experiences. Thus, even though asking clients what their counselling was like for them may appear to be an obvious and highly common-sense course of action to anyone outside the world of counselling, it can be seen that it threatens some of the most fundamental assumptions held by counsellors about the nature of their craft, and by researchers about the nature of their enterprise.

In addition, it is also essential to recognise that there are serious ethical and practical difficulties involved in doing research of this kind. Thus, for example, the researcher would be wary of interfering with the ongoing process of counselling or therapy, in case this were to have a detrimental effect on the client. Similarly, probing the experiences of clients who have completed counselling carries the risk of re-awakening unresolved issues. Counsellor–client confidentiality can also make it difficult to contact a representative sample of clients since the researcher would have to rely on the counsellor giving permission, and indeed making the initial approach to clients to invite their participation in the research.

Nevertheless, some research into client experience of counselling and psychotherapy has managed to overcome these obstacles. This review only attempts to discuss research in which an investigator has used some kind of standard research technique to explore client experiences, and has then analysed and drawn conclusions from this material. There are available a number of published autobiographical accounts of the experience of being in counselling, but these tend to consist of descriptive material alone, with no effort made to identify themes or general conclusions. Because of space restrictions, no attempt has been made to include a review of such autobiographical accounts in this chapter.

Studies of the Client's Experience of Counselling

The earliest studies of the client's experience were carried out by Rogers and his colleagues at the University of Chicago in the late 1940s (Axline, 1950; Lipkin, 1948, 1954; Rogers, 1951). In this research, clients of client-centred counselling wrote accounts of their experiences after the termination of counselling, or kept journal records during counselling.

The next piece of research to focus on client experiencing was conducted by Strupp and his colleagues at the University of North Carolina in the 1960s (Strupp et al., 1964, 1969). In these studies, 166 former psychotherapy patients at the University out-patient clinic completed a fairly lengthy (89-item) questionnaire which was mainly designed to assess their perceptions of their therapists and their evaluation of the effectiveness of their treatment. There were a few questions which allowed respondents to offer descriptions of their perceptions of the therapy in their own words. Their therapists also completed a questionnaire, and clinical records were consulted.

The research by Mayer and Timms (1970) was the first study to use interviews to find out about client experiences of counselling. Mayer and Timms interviewed sixty-one clients who had received counselling from the Family Welfare Association in London. The majority of the clients were working-class women. A primary aim of the research was to contrast the experiences of clients who were satisfied with their help with those who were dissatisfied. The Mayer and Timms research stimulated a lot of interest, partly because of the sometimes dramatic disjunction between client and counsellor expectations and assumptions which were revealed, and partly because it demonstrated that research on clients conducted by 'outsiders' was feasible. There followed a series of other interview studies. Maluccio (1979), in probably the most thorough exploration of client experience to date, interviewed thirty-three former clients and their counsellors from a Catholic Family Service Agency 'located in an urban area in the Northeastern United States'. Brannen and Collard (1982) carried out forty-eight interviews with people who had been counselled on marital problems either by Marriage Guidance or by a hospital-based counselling service in London. Oldfield (1983) carried out an interview and questionnaire study of fifty-two clients of the Isis Centre, a general counselling agency in Oxford. Markova et al. (1984) interviewed forty-seven patients with haemophilia, and twenty-nine carriers of haemophilia, about their experiences of genetic counselling. Timms and Blampied (1985) interviewed fifty clients from Marriage Guidance and Catholic Marriage Advisory Council offices in the northeast of England. Finally, Hunt (1985) interviewed fifty-one former clients of Manchester Marriage Guidance Council.

Valuable though these pieces of research based on interview methods have been, they all suffer from the limitation of relying wholly on retrospective accounts offered of events and experiences in counselling which might have taken place months previously. For this reason, some researchers have been attracted to a research technique called Interpersonal Process Recall (IPR), which enables clients to 're-live' the experience of individual counselling sessions. IPR was developed by Kagan et al. (1963), initially as an aid in counsellor training. The technique involves taking an audio- or video-tape record of a counselling session, then asking the counsellor or the client to listen to the tape and to stop it at any point of his or her own choice to comment on what he or she was experiencing during that moment of the counselling session. The interviewer may facilitate recall by asking open-ended questions. It is typically found that the IPR procedure is able to help people to re-enter their experience effectively, and to produce detailed accounts of their moment-by-moment thoughts and feelings during a counselling session. This method has been used in studies of client experiencing of counselling in a number of studies by Elliot and his colleagues at the University of Toledo (see Elliot, 1986 for a recent summary of this work) and by Rennie (1987) at York University, Ontario.

Studies using Interpersonal Process Recall generate fascinating, rich, complex descriptions of the experience of counselling. However, an inevitable consequence of the high degree of authenticity and immediacy of this material is that it is necessarily hard to categorise and interpret. An approach to understanding client experience of individual sessions which is much more structured and yields quantitative data has been developed by Orlinsky and Howard at the University of Chicago and Northwestern University. A major aim of the research carried out by Orlinsky and Howard (1986) has been to explore 'the psychological interior of psychotherapy', and to do this they devised a questionnaire which clients complete immediately after a session. The questionnaire, which takes 10–15 minutes to answer, asks clients to rate their feelings about how satisfied they were with the session, their relationship with the counsellor, their motivation to come to the next session and similar topics. Since the beginning of Orlinsky and Howard's research programme in 1965, client ratings on many thousands of sessions have been gathered. This information has been processed through the statistical technique of factor analysis, which allows conclusions to be drawn about patterns and regularities in the data.

Finally, open-ended questionnaires have been used by Feifel and Eells (1963) in a study of sixty-three clients in psychodynamic therapy and by Llewelyn (1988) in a study of twenty-two clients in eclectic therapy.

It can be seen, therefore, that a variety of different research methods have been used to study the client's experience of counselling and psychotherapy, including written journal records of individual sessions, tape-assisted recall, interviews and questionnaires. Also, a variety of units of experience have been studied: counselling as a whole, individual sessions and moments in sessions. Finally, a wide array of different types of clients (University Clinic, Marriage Counselling, Social Work Agency) receiving different types of counselling has been investigated. The variety of methods, units of study and client populations makes it difficult to arrive with confidence at general conclusions about the nature of the client experience of counselling. It is as though we are trying to construct a large, ambitious mosaic, but only in possession of a handful of tesserae. As a result, the discussion of client experience offered below must be treated with caution. After all, a few years ago, Smith et al. (1980) were able to review 475 studies of the *effectiveness* of therapy. When the number of studies of the *experience* of counselling or therapy approaches that figure, it will be possible to be much less tentative about what it can be like for clients to take part in this process.

The Nature of the Client's Experience

In the account of client experience which follows, no attempt has been made to summarise the conclusions of specific studies in turn. Instead, the aim has been to identify themes and observations which are found in more than one piece of research, and which might therefore seem to possess some general validity. Following the analysis suggested by Maluccio (1979), the client experience of counselling has been divided into three broad phases: becoming a client, the middle phase and ending. These phases will be discussed in turn.

Becoming a Client

The experience of becoming a client begins long before the person first meets his or her counsellor or therapist. There would appear to be a number of possible events which can occur on the route into counselling which can significantly influence the later experiences of the client. Thus, for example, the person entering counselling may have previously tried to solve his or her problem through the assistance of informal channels such as talking to friends or family members, 'unofficial' counsellors such as hairdressers or bartenders, or by writing to Agony Aunts in magazines. Mayer and Timms (1970) found that many of the clients they interviewed had not confided their problem to anyone else, even though there were other people close to them who would probably have responded sympathetically. Mayer and Timms (1970: 39) suggested that the norms, prevalent in western society, which 'enjoin individuals to be self-reliant rather than dependent on others', often make it difficult for people to seek help. One of their interviewees stated: 'I believe that what goes on in my house is my and my husband's business.' An informant in Brannen and Collard's (1982) study reflected the same basic attitude in saying: 'I believe if you can't solve your own problems then no one else can.'

One possible consequence of entering counselling from a background of 'normative constraint' regarding help-seeking is that the person may feel embarrassed, or ashamed about being a client: 'it was a sort of bitter thing of confessing my own inadequacy to have to come here' (Timms and Blampied, 1985: 19); 'I feel a little ashamed to be in psychotherapy. . . . I think I must be feeling that I'm weak or something' (Fitts, 1965: 80). Timms and Blampied (1985) found that two-thirds of their sample reported feelings of shame associated with entering marital counselling.

Other reasons for failing to get effective help before entering counselling that have been reported in the literature are:

— belief that others were unable or unwilling to help;
— unwillingness to burden others;
— lack of trust in possible confidants;
— not saying anything because 'if I told my family *anything* about it I would have to tell them *all* about it';
— previous ineffective or unacceptable advice from confidants.

These findings are derived from the studies carried out by Mayer and Timms (1970), Brannen and Collard (1982) and Timms and Blampied (1985). One conclusion which can be drawn from these studies is that people entering counselling have often either tried to get help from non-professional sources, or have seriously considered that possibility. In doing so, they have made judgements about the helpfulness or otherwise of the responses they have received and, in then turning to a professional, trained counsellor or psychotherapist, are expecting a different quality of assistance. It is not surprising, therefore, that in their early contact with the counsellor, clients are evaluating that person. It is as though they are asking themselves: '*Is this a person who can help me?*'

Direct evidence for the notion that the client's first experience of the counsellor is one in which the helper is being heavily evaluated as a potential source of assistance can be found particularly in the interviews carried out by Maluccio (1979: 124). He observed: 'especially noteworthy was the frequency with which clients offered evaluative comments regarding the worker's competence'. Positive statements of counsellor competence were: 'knew what he was doing'; 'had put it all together' and 'always had the situation well in hand'. Negative evaluations were expressed in phrases such as: 'didn't know much more than I did'; 'too young, new, inexperi- enced' and 'disorganised'.

Clients' ideas about what constitutes competence can, however, be at odds with the assumptions of their helpers. This point is mentioned in virtually all the interview studies, but is emphasised most clearly in Mayer and Timms (1970) and Hunt (1985). Mayer and Timms write about the 'clash in perspective' between the mainly working-class clients in their study and their counsellors. They report that the *dissatisfied* clients they interviewed had been looking for expert diagnosis, advice, recommendations and action to resolve the problem. One dissatisfied client, for example, said: 'I realised that she [the counsellor] wasn't entering into what I was saying at all.... . She just wasn't giving me an answer or any advice at all.' In the Hunt (1985) study of Marriage Guidance clients, the theme of advice-giving emerges as a strong difference in orientation between clients and counsellors. One respondent, for instance, said: '[I] thought that somebody would hand me a solution on a plate . . . I thought there would be a set kind of plan on how to solve our problems.' (p. 34). Hunt notes that some clients who initially come looking for advice can subsequently change their ideas about the nature of counselling, and the issue of how clients experience differences or difficulties in relation to counsellors will be discussed more fully later in this chapter. For the moment, however, it can be seen that the 'clash of perspective' which frequently exists between counsellor and client illustrates the evaluative quality of the initial encounter with the professional helper. It is not so much that the client has a well defined set of expectations which are brought to the counselling agency like an interpersonal shopping-list. In fact the client recorded in Brannen and Collard (1982: 172) as stating that 'I didn't really know what to expect. . . . I really had no idea — no experience to go on', is fairly typical. It seems, instead, more as though the help-seeker arrives with a vague and general question — 'is this someone who can help?' — and then finds that various unconscious or taken-for-granted assumptions about what counts as helping may emerge as problematic in the first few sessions. It is important to acknowledge that studies in this area suggest that a 'clash of perspective' of some kind is an experience which is common in all groups of clients investigated, and is not restricted to working-class clients alone.

Another significant influence which has its origins in the time before entering counselling is the person's previous experience of helping. It would appear that clients who have been counselled before will often make assumptions about the new counsellor based on their experience of the previous one. It may also be that the counsellor is experienced as similar to a non-professional person whom the client has previously known to be supportive or helpful. Maluccio (1979: 131), for example, found that clients frequently referred to their counsellors in ways such as: 'she was like a mother'; 'he was always there, like a good father' or 'she was like a good friend'. Timms and Blampied (1985) used the phrase 'formal friend' to capture the sense that many of their informants had of their relationships with their counsellors.

Finally, it should be noted that most clients describe their emotional state in the first session in terms such as 'tense', 'anxious' or 'nervous'. However, this level of distress is often not revealed to the counsellor during the first session. The client is not yet sure of the counsellor, and may therefore keep many of these feelings hidden (Hunt, 1985: 31). One interesting by-product of this process is that, when counsellors and clients are asked to talk about their experiences of the first session, the counsellor is more likely to recollect the problems and issues which the client presented, and the client is more likely to remember the feelings they had and their reactions to the helper (Maluccio, 1979: 61).

The conclusion of the phase of becoming a client appears to be marked by two main processes. The first aspect consists of reaching a mutual agreement over how client and counsellor are going to work together. This is achieved by discussing expectations of each other, and defining ground rules such as the length and frequency of sessions, confidentiality, payment, and so on. There is evidence, from Maluccio (1979) and Gaunt (1985), that when this kind of 'contract-forming' (whether formal or informal) does not take place in the first session, or at least very early on in therapy, the client may feel confused and rejected, or may believe that the counsellor is not interested in him or her, and can therefore be unwilling to return for another meeting.

The second process, which occurs in parallel with the construction of a contract, is more concerned with empathy and the client's belief that the counsellor or therapist can appreciate how he or she feels about things. The sense of this is captured well in Hobson's (1985) idea of a 'feeling-language', a way of talking or being together which is personal, in which there is exchange or dialogue, and which is about feelings. It is probably very difficult for clients to articulate clearly what this experience is like for them, particularly in interviews conducted many weeks or months after it occurred. Thus, for example, a client interviewed by Mayer and Timms (1970: 84) said: 'I sort of felt, well, somebody understands and they're interested and they want to help and they don't think it's silly.'

An instance of the actual growth of this kind of emotional connectedness can be found in the section in Rogers (1951: 89–94) where he examines a client's account of her experience of a first counselling session. At the beginning of the session, the client talks about herself and her feelings, but experiences the counsellor as a 'mirror'. But 'a mirror image isn't sufficient . . . in a sense I am already familiar with that through private reflections'. Then . . . 'you made the reflection that struck the spark . . . it's as if a charge had gradually accumulated in my futile attempts to establish an emotional flow, and finally it reached sufficient strength to jump the gap'. What has happened is that the counsellor has found the right words or gestures to take the first step in building a mutual 'feeling-language', and the 'emotional flow' between counsellor and client can begin.

The phase of becoming a client can then be considered to culminate in what Maluccio (1979: 62) has called the experience of 'establishing an emotional connection'. This experience seems to mark the transition between evaluating the counsellor, and finally deciding to 'work' with him or her, and can perhaps be summed up in the words of a client interviewed by Maluccio (1979: 62): 'some kind of bond grew between us . . . [he] seemed like someone I had known for a long time, even though I had never met him before'. Once this happens, client and counsellor are ready to enter the next stage.

The Middle Phase of Counselling

The previous section has reviewed some of the research material on the client's experience of entering counselling. It was seen that the experience of becoming a client is one in which the person's sense of the present relationship with the counsellor or psychotherapist is very much anchored in his or her experience of how he or she got there, and in his or her assumptions and expectations about the nature of helping. It was also noted that it is necessary for the counsellor and client to construct an emotional bond and to have some agreement over how they are to work together. This whole process can happen very quickly, as with the client just described by Rogers (1951), or it can take a great deal of time and effort by both parties. On some occasions a good enough relationship is never created, and although clients may pretend that one does exist to 'save face' (Maluccio, 1979: 68), counselling in these cases is rarely satisfactory or effective. But what happens for clients if and when the beginning phase is successfully completed? What are the experiences that clients report in the middle phase of counselling, after they have really started but before they have become too aware of the possibility of ending?

There is clearly a lot happening in the middle phase of therapy or counselling, and much of the time it is all happening at once. It is difficult, therefore, to capture in words the sense of what this experience is like as a whole for clients. However, from the research literature it appears that there can be identified three central aspects of the client's experiencing at this stage. These aspects are: the experience of self, the experience of the relationship and the experience of significant or helpful events.

The Experience of Self   The client's experience of self is of course powerfully affected by the relationship with the counsellor, and by the helping process. However, it also seems that, for most clients, the middle phase of therapy or counselling is a time when the focus of their attention is primarily on themselves. Counselling sessions represent occasions for inner exploration. Rennie (1984, 1985a, b, 1987) has presented a number of analyses of Interpersonal Process Recall interviews conducted with thirteen clients soon after they had emerged from a therapy session. These clients were asked, in interviews which lasted for between one and four hours, to describe their experiences in the session by commenting on an audio-tape recording of it.

One important observation which Rennie makes in this research is that the clients experienced themselves as being aware that there were definite themes in what they talked about in sessions. These themes related to dilemmas or issues concerning their sense of self — their feelings and ideas about who they were. Examples were: 'my worries about being a student', and 'my feelings about my girl-friend sleeping with someone else'. This observation is perhaps an obvious one to make, but Rennie (1984) reports on two additional aspects of this experience: the client experiences his or her exploration of the theme as having a sense of direction, or *track*, and the client may often experience two or more themes or tracks at the same time.

What is being suggested is that the person enters a counselling session with a sense of a problem or issues they want to do something about (what Maluccio (1979: 70) terms the 'problem focus'), and then 'the client develops a train of thought related to [the problem] . . . he has a sense of being on a track, that where he is at this moment is somehow connected to the disturbance and promises to lead into deeper aspects of it . . . the client recedes deeper into himself' (Rennie, 1984: 11). Different clients may want different kinds of response from the therapist or counsellor at this point. For some, any interruption will threaten to dislodge them from their track, for others the prompting and reflecting activities of the counsellor are helpful in enabling them to keep to the track. However, clients seem to be aware (at least in retrospect) of when the conversation has shifted from their track on to one defined by the counsellor.

One way in which some of the clients in Rennie's studies explored a track was through telling stories about events which occurred some time before the therapy session. Rennie (1985a) uses the term 'narratives' to describe these stories, and describes his own scepticism, as a therapist, about the value of story-telling, seeing it as potentially an avoidance of 'real' therapeutic work. He was surprised to find in his research, then, that for the clients he was interviewing, there was much more going on under the surface than would have been readily apparent to a listening counsellor or therapist. Clients used story-telling to deal with feelings of residual tension about the events they were describing, to re-enter difficult areas of feeling, and stimulate a wider network of thoughts and images associated with the event. What the counsellor hears is the story, but what the client is experiencing is much more complex. There are covert or hidden dimensions to the narrative, which the client is continuously choosing to articulate or to keep quiet about. A client may for example construct a particular narrative in order to present him- or herself to the counsellor in a favourable light; or the client may be in touch with a quickly changing stream of inner processes which would be interrupted and lost if explained to the counsellor.

As Rennie describes it, the experience of being a client at this stage in therapy is one of following tracks, some of which are explicitly put into words and some of which are not. Rennie (1987: 8) writes that, in the reports of his research informants: 'There is a compellingness to the track, clients feel that they are on the edge of their experience, there is uncertainty whether words can be found to express what they are sensing, and this is associated with feelings of tantalisation and excitement.' From time to time, however, they will 'catch themselves' in this process. Either it occurs to them that the track being followed is not productive, or they encounter a threatening thought or feeling, or the counsellor says something which throws them off the track. When any of these things happen, the client is moved off the unreflective, 'raw' experiencing of the track, and becomes involved in consciously monitoring or choosing what to do or where to go next. The experience of the client can therefore be understood as following a rhythm of 'raw' self-immersion along unexplored tracks, followed by times of reflection and monitoring.

One of the common factors in all forms of counselling and therapy is the expectation that the client will confront, explore and work through previously avoided thoughts and feelings. As a result, one frequent consequence of the 'tracking' already described is that the client experiences personal material that is at or beyond the edge of that with which he or she is comfortable. Thus, one client in Fitts's (1965) study wrote of therapy as 'a trip through Hell'; and a client interviewed by Hunt (1985) talked about 'feeling dismantled' during this phase of his counselling. In the large-scale survey of client experience of therapy conducted by Orlinsky and Howard (1986), clients reported high levels of feeling during sessions, with the emotions of anxiety and relief being prominent.

At times, the track the client is following leads to places which are so new for the client that it is difficult for him or her to retrieve them again or keep them in awareness. Thus, for example, a client wrote for Rogers (1951: 100) that, after a therapy session:

> . . . odd thoughts and insights have flashed into consciousness . . . sometimes they have been quite clear . . . but then quite suddenly they are gone and I can't even remember what they were . . . there is one insight that crops up again and again, but I can't for the life of me think what it is.

Eventually, when the client has been able to assimilate new feelings and understandings, there is a sense that the self has changed, and this experience can be marked by feelings of confidence (Orlinsky and Howard, 1986) or pride, as illustrated in the statement made by a man in Fitts's (1965) study: 'I think to myself, "man, it's good to know that I've licked that problem". . . . I do feel proud at these times that I'm in therapy.'

Thus, the experience of self in the middle phase of counselling is characterised by exploration, discovery and change, and a rhythm of immersion in self followed by reflection. All this is, of course, taking place within the context of a relationship with a helper, and is dependent on the quality of that relationship.

The Experience of Relationship The importance of the experience of relationship is one of the strongest themes to emerge from studies of the client's experience of therapy or counselling. Orlinsky and Howard (1986: 492), for example, found in their research that in something like three-quarters of the sessions studied, clients perceived the relationship with their therapists as 'vivid, mutually receptive, sensitively collaborative, liberal and open, and mutually affirming'. For counsellors, this result, with its sense of what the authors label 'healing magic', is very encouraging. However, both Orlinsky and Howard and other researchers also report that there are a number of more problematic aspects of the experience of 'relatedness' to a therapist or counsellor, which occur with some frequency. In the Orlinsky and Howard (1986) study, for instance, three ways in which clients sometimes appeared to perceive the relationship were described as 'ambivalent nurturance-dependence', 'defensive impasse' and 'conflictual erotisation'. In the first of these patterns, the client experienced him- or herself 'courting a therapist who is seen as rejecting'. In the second, the therapist is experienced as 'mean and attacking'. In the third, the client experience is one of sexual arousal in the presence of a therapist who is uncertain as to how to react.

It is of some significance that the relationship themes which emerged in the large-scale questionnaire survey conducted by Orlinsky and Howard (1986) are also apparent in the responses of individual clients interviewed in more intensive, 'in-depth' studies. The perception and experience of the therapeutic relationship as 'healing magic' is found in the words of a Marriage Guidance client interviewed by Hunt (1985), who described the relationship as a 'safe place', or a 'lifeline', or the person who wrote for Fitts (1965) that 'I was having a wonderful time in therapy — thoroughly enjoying the freedom, the understanding, and the acceptance'.

The less positive or comfortable elements in the client's experience of the relationship have also been uncovered by other researchers. On occasions clients clearly feel that they and their counsellor or therapist are not on the same wavelength at all. Hunt (1985), for example, asked counselling clients to rate their perceptions of how their counsellors were in the relationship. Although these clients agreed that their helpers were 'attentive', 'genuine' and 'accepting', there was less support for the statement 'I felt the counsellor understood my feelings'.

Perhaps the most penetrating analysis of discordance in the therapy or counselling relationship has been offered by Rennie (1985b) in his study of client *deference*. As we have seen, Rennie characterises the client experience in general as one in which the person is often aware of much more than they choose to communicate to the therapist: 'clients reported that, busy as they were verbally with the therapist, they were even busier in their minds' (Rennie, 1987: 10). The experience of deference occurs when this internal activity is devoted to working out how to make a good impression with the therapist. An example Rennie (1985b) offers is of a student in therapy who was telling the therapist about his inability to study. The therapist asked the client in the session how much he had been studying. The client replied 'a half-hour a day'. Seeking clarification, the therapist then said 'you mean, a half-hour a day per course', to which the client said 'yes'. In the later Interpersonal Process Recall interview, the client admitted to Rennie that he had lied, because 'he had not wanted to look foolish in the eyes of the therapist'.

Rennie et al. (1988) have referred to this kind of incident in terms of the *politics* of the therapy relationship. It is a relationship in which one member is an expert, is on home territory and appears to be in control. It is of interest here that although most of the clients in the Orlinsky and Howard (1986) research felt positively about their therapists, they nevertheless experienced themselves as only taking the initiative to a moderate extent, and being very receptive to any initiative taken by the therapist. Rennie (1985b: 15) observed that clients in his study were 'extremely reluctant to disclose their disenchantments with their therapists to their therapists'. Instead, when there was a misunderstanding on the part of the therapist, the clients sometimes withdrew a little and witheld important information.

Taking as a whole the conclusions of researchers who have studied the experience of relationship in the middle phase of counselling or therapy, the strongest theme to emerge is that of *ambivalence*. The counsellor is seen as expert and helpful, but also as someone who misses the point. The counsellor is a person with whom to be honest, but also someone whose approval is sometimes sought by less-than-honest means.

The Experience of Significant or Helpful Events   A fair amount of research has focussed on the question of what the client in counselling experiences as *helpful* or as *hindering*. In one typical study, Murphy et al. (1984) interviewed twenty-four out-patients receiving cognitive-behavioural psychotherapy from clinical psychologists. These clients were able to identify a large number of factors which they believed had been helpful to their progress in therapy. The most frequently cited factors, endorsed by over half of this sample of clients, were:

— getting advice from the therapist;
— talking to someone interested in my problems;
— encouragement and reassurance;
— talking to someone who understands;
— the instillation of hope;
— self-understanding.

Other studies which have asked clients what they have found helpful have arrived at similar conclusions (for example, Hunt, 1985; Mayer and Timms, 1970; Strupp et al., 1964). There is some evidence that the experience of catharsis or emotional release is also frequently experienced as helpful (see Hunt, 1985; Mayer and Timms, 1970). It may be that the restriction of the Murphy et al. (1984) study to clients receiving a cognitively oriented therapy may have led these researchers to underestimate the importance of this factor. Llewelyn (1988) found that the experience most frequently found to be helpful by clients in eclectic psychotherapy was that of problem-solving. In the Timms and Blampied (1985) and Hunt (1985) studies of marital counselling, a number of clients said that they found it helpful that the counselling sessions were 'official conversations' between them and their spouses. The counselling setting forced both partners to 'put their cards on the table' in a way that they had not found possible in private.

In a study of clients' perceptions of what hindered progress in therapy, Lietaer and Neirinck (1987) asked clients in client-centred therapy to write down immediately after each session their impressions of what might have hindered progress in that session. Three main types of hindering event emerged from their analysis of these accounts. First, clients felt that things went badly when they did not co-operate with the therapist by being silent, by talking superficially or by not daring to talk about some things. Secondly, problems in the relationship between therapist and client were seen as a hindrance (for example, the therapist not being warm enough, confronting too much or too little, not valuing or accepting the client enough). Thirdly, clients found it unhelpful when their therapists made interventions which took them off their own 'track', when the therapist said things that 'did not feel right'.

There is fairly high level of agreement among different studies concerning the factors which clients find helpful or unhelpful. Also, some studies (for example Llewelyn and Hume, 1979) show that what clients find helpful are general processes such as 'having someone to talk to' or 'getting advice', rather than specific therapeutic techniques such as systematic desensitisation or dream analysis. This state of affairs has encouraged some writers on therapy to conclude that there exists a set of 'nonspecific' helpful factors, common to all forms of therapy (see Wills (1982) for a review of the literature on this topic).

Perhaps one of the most intriguing findings in this whole area is the perception by many clients that *advice* from their counsellors or therapists is highly valued, and the absence of advice is seen as unhelpful or uncaring. This result is particularly striking given the fact that most counsellors and therapists would portray themselves as reluctant or unwilling to give advice. There appears to be a difference, however, between what clients experience as advice-giving, and the way that a counsellor or therapist would perceive the same intervention. Maluccio (1979: 76), for example, reports one client as talking about the advice she received in the following words: '. . . I was trying to do too much at the same time . . . [the therapist] advised me to choose one or two goals to concentrate on at one time . . .' It is unlikely that a therapist would categorise this as 'advice', classifying it instead as an instance of problem-solving, or offering structure. In addition, to add to the complexity of this issue, in a study of genetic counselling Markova et al. (1984) found marked differences between clients concerning their wishes for advice from a counsellor.

To sum up the conclusions of research into the client's experience during the middle phase of counselling or therapy is difficult; there are a number of different patterns of experiencing which have been reported in the literature. Some of the more salient themes, nevertheless, appear to be a sense of self-directed self-exploration, periods of ambivalence and a struggle to retain a sense of relatedness to the helper. It is in the light of these challenges and difficulties that Maluccio (1979) rightly characterises the key task during this period as that of *staying* engaged in the therapeutic process.

The Final Phase: Ending
There are several different ways in which a counselling relationship may come to an end. Termination may be mutual or unilateral; it may be planned or spontaneous; it may be decided by the client or by the counsellor; or it can be the result of action by an outside agency. Ending may be in response to success or in acknowledge-ment of failure. These different routes in all probability mean different things to clients, but research into this aspect of the client experience has yet to explore the precise implications of the varieties of ending.

Maluccio (1979: 92) quotes a number of clients who have under-gone successful therapy as expressing such feelings and attitudes towards the ending as: 'it was a traumatic experience', 'I felt like losing a lifelong friend' and 'it was like losing an arm you no longer needed'. The main themes in these accounts are emotional investment and dependence on the counsellor, ambivalence about ending and an awareness of impending loss of support. Maluccio (1979) reports that the clients he interviewed who had found less benefit in therapy, and who experienced unplanned endings, 'were more likely to deny having any feelings about termination'. Hunt (1985) observed that a number of the clients in her study were surprised that counselling had been brought to a close when it had, and reported feelings of 'unfinished business' as a result. In this research there was also a significant minority of clients who felt aggrieved or angry at the end, because they felt themselves to have been 'let down' by the counsellor or the agency. Indeed, Hunt (1985: 67) reported that one client had accepted her invitation to take part in the research 'because she still felt so angry and wanted to complain'. Timms and Blampied (1985) found that one aspect of ending for a number of clients was that, towards the end, they began to experience the sessions as more 'social' and less serious. One indicator of this transition was that the client began to take more interest in the counsellor as a person rather than as someone playing a professional role.

The study of the client's experience of ending is a fertile area for further research. As Maluccio (1979: 92) puts it, 'becoming disengaged is in some ways more complicated than becoming engaged'. Yalom's (1966) follow-up study of therapy group drop-outs reveals the wide range of factors involved in unplanned endings, and hints at how much more there is to be learned about the dynamics of endings.

Conclusions

Counsellors and psychotherapists sooner or later learn to accommo-date themselves to their role, they come to take for granted the phenomenon of a stranger opening up to them. For clients, however, the role is almost certainly a new one, and often their sense of what might happen or what should happen is very unclear. Research into the experience of being a client reveals many ways in which the client's experience is hidden from, or different to, that of the counsellor or therapist. It also suggests that there exists a deep ambivalence even in clients who see themselves as benefiting from counselling. The research which has been conducted, limited though it is, is surely of some practical value in offering practitioners insight into the way it looks from the other chair. It is also possible that research studies of this type might be particularly valuable exercises for therapists or counsellors in training, all the more so when compared with conventional quasi-experimental research designs which place the investigator in a supposedly objective, detached relationship with the 'subjects' of research.

It has also been suggested by Maluccio (1979) that research into the client experience may be useful for clients themselves. One of his respondents told him that the research interview helped her to 'gather her thoughts' and therefore make more sense for herself of what her therapy actually meant. He also reports on a number of workshops in which former clients have discussed their experiences with practitioners in training. This kind of event not only allows clients to feel valued and useful, but reminds professionals that the consumer is someone with strengths, skills and competencies as well as problems.

This review of the research literature has identified a number of areas of client experience which are ripe for further investigation, as well as a number of gaps in present knowledge. Further research is certainly needed on the meaning for clients of 'advice', and the way they make sense of and use different counsellor interventions which they see as 'advice-giving'. The studies reviewed, taken as a whole, suggest that, although there are common features in the experience of different kinds of counselling, there are also some real differences. At the present time, however, the practical significance of these differences cannot be clearly evaluated. In his major piece of research in this area, Maluccio (1979) consistently makes the point that therapists underestimate the impact which the rest of the client's life has on the changes which may appear to be associated with therapy. The therapist's experience of the client is mainly of someone whom he or she meets in an office perhaps once a week; the client's experience is of a life in which therapy plays its part, but only in relation to everything else.

It is clear that a variety of research methods and techniques has been used to study the client's experience, and that each has its characteristic strengths and weaknesses. The impression gained from reading the work in this field is that it would probably be useful for at least some future researchers to focus on rather more limited domains of experience than has hitherto been the case. The researchers who have, whether by interview or questionnaire, attempted to capture *all* of the sense or feeling of being a client have generally produced overwhelmingly complex sets of data, which are difficult to interpret. One yearns for sharper, more focussed and more digestible enquiries into topics such as the client's experience of the counsellor's 'tracking' or failure in tracking; the apparently paradoxical instances when the client conceals his or her true feelings in order to win the counsellor's approval or the ways in which clients make sense of different types of ending.

Ultimately, though, it must be acknowledged that any significant future development of research into the client's experience of counselling and psychotherapy may represent a radical intrusion into the professional domain. This is research which gives the client a voice. No longer would the client's view be filtered through the screen of scientific method. And who *really* knows where that might lead?

2 A Client's Experience of Failure

Laura Allen

Before Counselling

Perhaps people try to kill themselves to tell others how dead they are inside.

I had taken all the pills I could find around the flat. I did not know if it was enough — and I did not really care. I remember lying on my bed crying as incidents from early life came to mind. Strangely, these scenes from the past were all of happy events when I was a bouncy, joyous little girl of four or five. I recall an enormous desire to become that happy little girl again.

The next memory is of excruciating pain in my chest and bright lights which proved to be a hospital room. The first person to speak to me was a nurse of about my own age. She smiled and held my hand. I suppose she was just taking my pulse, but she felt so warm that I cried. The next two days in hospital were cold: medical people do not like suicide.

There was no counselling of any kind, but the hospital social worker suggested that I might seek that kind of help, so on my release I made enquiries through the Citizen's Advice Bureau. I was too scared and embarrassed to ask my own doctor for contacts. The CAB at first suggested I contact my doctor, but later came up with the phone number of an office which was used by a few psychotherapists or counsellors working in private practice. I kept the phone number in my handbag for two weeks until I realised that things were not improving: I was becoming more scared of living than of making that phone call. I did not know what to say on the phone and the first time I put the receiver down when the receptionist answered. I felt stupid, and knew that I had to ring again because this was my only chance, but I waited half an hour in case the receptionist realised that it was me who had phoned the first time. When I phoned back the receptionist was very polite. She gave me an appointment with a Dr Parker. To my surprise, I found myself asking if Dr Parker was a woman because I really would prefer to see a woman. The receptionist said that there were no women in the practice, and in any case I would be 'better with Dr

Parker'. A little voice deep inside me did not like this receptionist, but I was miles away from expressing that.

The First Counselling Experience

I spent ages getting myself ready for the first appointment with Dr Parker. When I looked at myself in the mirror I did not like what I saw: a twenty-eight-year-old woman with too much make-up. I washed it all off and looked again. Now I was more like myself — a haggard, lonely and 'hunted'-looking divorcee teacher of English who could have passed for forty. Now I looked as abused as I felt. The years of fear and guilt were etched on my face: fear of my father's beating, my mother's cruel tongue and my teachers' normal demands which I never seemed able to satisfy. And the guilt related to my father's leaving, my husband's leaving and my mother's blaming me for both.

I was incredibly nervous about this appointment. I arrived at the street twenty minutes early and walked around the block so many times that I thought I would be noticed. At last it was two minutes before the hour and I entered the building to be directed to a consulting room by a rather uninviting receptionist.

I wish therapists and counsellors could just imagine what it feels like for a client to come to a stranger for help when you feel this is your last hope.

He was very gracious as he directed me to a chair; it was some sessions later that I realised that *his* chair was higher than mine. Even then I was not sure — I wondered if I were imagining it — but one time I had a good look before we sat down, and sure enough, there was about 2-inches difference. It felt as though, no matter what I did, he would always be the superior one who had to be 'looked up to'.

I do not remember much of the content of our first two sessions. I know I told him my life story in more detail than ever before. He did not do much except put a few questions and say when the time was finished. At that time I did not know much about counselling, but I thought his behaviour was strange: I was giving so much of myself and he was acting as though he didn't care a damn.

At one point in our third meeting we had an exchange which I found so offensive that I think I can remember it more or less verbatim. It felt as though he was playing with me, but in a cruel way — like a little boy pulling the wings off a fly:

Me: I hope you won't think it's cheeky, but I was wondering if you had been doing this for a long time or whether you were a trainee counsellor?

Counsellor: What makes you interested in that?

Me: Well, it's just that I wasn't sure what you felt about what we were doing. I mean I don't mind if you *are* a trainee — everyone's got to be one sometime. . . . [*Silence*]

Me: Why won't you tell me?

Counsellor: Because it's not important to the work we're doing.

Me: But it *is* important to me — and really I don't mind if you are a trainee. . . .

Counsellor: Well, if you don't mind either way, then it doesn't matter, does it? [*Silence*]

Things went from bad to worse. He played his silly games — I really think that he *tried* to be detached and authoritarian. Having read about it since, I suppose he was trying to arouse *transference* in me. But he did that without even waiting to find out how desperate my problem was and whether that was appropriate. As it was, I was really bad. A good metaphor for what I felt was that I was walking around with no skin. Actually, by calling it a metaphor, I am implying more sanity than was the case, because at times I *literally* felt without skin and experienced the physical pain that might go with that. I was feeling as vulnerable as that and he gave me absolutely nothing. I think just one smile and cuddle would have melted me — it would have brought such peace. Instead, the way he treated me was just a more subtle version of the abuse I had already had in my life. My father had been cruel to me in a physical way, by beating me, but this man did not even need to touch me to bully me. He did not respond to anything I said, so I gradually shut up. During one session neither of us said anything at all — not one word! I was incredibly scared. Certainly, transference was happening: I had what might be called an irrational fear that if I said or did anything he would hurt me in some way. This mirrored what I had felt as a child, but it was also *real*, there and then, because he *did* punish me with coldness so many times: I smiled at him and he continued to look back coldly; I begged him to help me when I thought I was going to die and he looked back coldly. One time I remember that I was writhing about on the floor — I was shit scared — I thought that I was dying. It is difficult to describe, but I really thought I was dying there and then on his floor. I reached out to him and tried to speak but I was mute. I just could not utter any words. He moved back in his seat and I saw his eyes flicker nervously.

During our next session he spoke more than he had done in all of our previous meetings. He spoke about how difficult I was finding life at the moment and that I might consider admitting myself as a voluntary patient to the local psychiatric hospital. He knew a psychiatrist who worked there and it would be easy to arrange. I felt devastated. Although I disliked the way he was with me I had kept coming in blind faith that some miracle might happen. I had not stopped because I knew that this was my last chance. Now he was dumping me — he was, in effect, saying 'Go on, kill yourself.' I knew about psychiatric hospitals and I was not going to die there.

My devastation quickly gave way to anger and for the first time since childhood it came out uncensored, as I said: 'You fucking bastard . . . you bastard . . . you fucking cruel bastard.' I kicked over his coffee table and stormed out of the office. I stopped at his receptionist, threw four £5 notes at her, and said that she should do something obscene to her boss with the receipt.

I hope counsellors and therapists do not try to take credit for all the healthy changes which happen to take place in their clients. I hope Dr Parker never finds out that his sadism triggered my fury and eventually led to my recovery. When I got back to my flat I did not burst into tears as might usually happen. Instead, I stormed around mouthing things to him like 'You're not going to destroy me you bastard.' Other times that I had been hurt I had blamed myself and compounded that hurt with guilt. Now I was hurt — but I was *angry* — in a funny way I felt tremendous. I strutted around the house savouring the question of whether I would report him to the British Medical Association or burn his office down, or both! Depression followed later, but I think it was not as hopeless as it might have been without that anger.

Looking back on this experience after some years and having read a couple of books about counselling, my assessment of Dr Parker is that he was magnificent at *developing the transference* but clueless as to what to do with it. Another criticism is that it felt as though he had his way of going about things and he just went ahead with that regardless of who was sitting in the other chair. I also think there were a few times that he was positively *scared* of me, which is not very helpful when the client is full of fear herself. I think he probably *was* a trainee, but that is not sufficient excuse. For a trainee to behave so *powerfully* seems highly dangerous. Also, I cannot escape the feeling that, as a person, regardless of his counselling role, he was a *bully* — there was a coldness about him that was more than an act. I hope that he is not still practising. In fact, as I have been recalling these events, I have regretted that I did not take action against Dr Parker at the time. I wonder how many women clients he has had since that time.

The Second Experience

I was in less of a crisis a year later when I sought help through a voluntary counselling agency. The only reason I went to the voluntary sector was to find a woman. All the private avenues I explored turned out to be men and I was not having one of them after the last time!

At the first appointment the counsellor came to the door to meet me, shook my hand and introduced herself as 'Mary Hopkins'. Suddenly, my previous counselling experience flashed before me and I came out in a cold sweat as I realised, for the first time, that I did not know the Christian name of my previous counsellor! I had been with him through all that abuse and I believe he never divulged his first name. I remember that this sudden realisation made me feel sick — it felt like being raped.

I found myself nervously talking and crying about this experience in that first session with Mary. She was very warm and sympathetic and that was nice for me. She also said she was angry at my previous counsellor and that helped too.

It was a relief to be with Mary and things went very smoothly except over the question of money. Her counselling organisation invited donations, so I paid exactly what I had done in my previous contract, which was £20 per session. I was earning only an average income as a teacher, but it was important for me to feel that I was serious about doing this counselling work and paying was part of that. However, when I offered this as my contribution at the end of the first session, Mary looked shocked and said that people usually paid only about £3. I explained that paying a professional fee was important to me and if she took my money, it might, in a sense, help to balance the lower contribution of some other person. She took it but looked most uneasy, and walked me back through to the receptionist whom she asked to give me a receipt, which I didn't really want.

Mary was well organised about the money in later sessions, having these unwanted receipts made out in advance, but she always looked uneasy when I handed the money to her. Perhaps it was made worse by the fact that I liked to pay in notes rather than by cheque. I told her that for me this emphasised the commitment I was making, but I think she did not really understand.

Mary was warm and soft — a very caring person. I imagine she would have been a lovely mother as long as the child did nothing wrong. It was certainly comforting for me to be with her and perhaps I needed a bit of that warmth after the first cold experience of counselling.

However, the honest assessment must be that this was also an experience of failure. I realised after only a few sessions that Mary was limited in what she could tolerate. When I got into my really desperate 'lost' crying she would try to take me out of it with some version of '*there, there, it will be alright*'. That stopped me crying and helped to get me really stuck. Sometimes she looked anxious and embarked upon long stories about 'young people' she had known who had eventually 'found their way'. I tried to tell her that I did not need reassurance like this — that I had survived much more desperate experiences. But she just looked embarrassed about failing me. I wonder how often clients 'look after' their counsellors, because I did that a bit with Mary. I found myself repeatedly avoiding the expressions of feeling and confrontations which I knew would be problematic for her.

Mary cuddled me a few times in our early sessions and then she stopped. I think this was actually quite sensitive of her because I would probably have had to ask her not to do it. This may sound strange to the reader who remembers my desperate wish for my first counsellor to hold me, but it reflects the different state I was in — now I was not *so* desperately scared that I craved *any* holding. Certainly, the right kind of physical contact might have been good, but with Mary it felt strange. It is difficult to describe how it felt but it was as though she needed to hold me more than I needed to be held.

Nothing much really happened in counselling with Mary. I felt that although she was warm I did not get any closer to her than to my first counsellor, though any comparison with him is unfair since Mary was at least kind. In entering counselling this second time I had hoped to make real progress in understanding myself better and perhaps gain in confidence because of that. I think I was really ready to work: all I needed was someone who could stay with me and be untroubled by my trouble. Mary was not that person and while it would be easy to let the kind, well meaning Marys of this world off the hook, I really think that selection and training, even for voluntary counselling, should manage to do better.

At the end of our penultimate session I asked Mary what approach to counselling she used. I was reading *Individual Therapy in Britain* (Dryden, 1984), and developing a fair understanding of the different methods. She said that she 'used her own way', which was 'eclectic', but which was 'mainly Rogerian'. I remember feeling disappointed because I knew that 'Rogerian' was the same as 'person-centred' and this was the approach in which I was most interested. If this was what person-centred counselling was, then perhaps there was nothing which would help me.

Later Reflections

One of the problems about being a client in a bad counselling or therapy experience is that you fear that you will not be believed — and when you feel vulnerable you are not sure if you believe yourself. Failing twice made me entertain the thought that *I* was causing the failures. But I really don't think that that was the case. Indeed, in a funny way, I wonder if perhaps I was actually closer to mental health than both of my helpers. It sounds a crazy thing to say, but while I have been writing this chapter I have considered the possibility that both of these helpers had pathologies which ran even deeper than mine. I certainly think that my first counsellor had found a profession which gave expression to his psychopathy, and perhaps the second needed to find a place to continue as a mother now that her children had grown up.

I am at present in the early stages of my third counselling experience, which is totally different from the first two. This time I only picked the counsellor after a detailed recommendation from a mutual friend and an exploratory first session during which I decided that this was a gentle man whom I could trust. Already I have found *hope* — I think I am now in a relationship in which I can be free yet not rejected, challenged yet accepted, and in which my counsellor is personally secure. The strength I am feeling from this is amazing.

It may seem strange to try again after two failures, but despite these, I know from what I have read that the process can work. Also, I recognise that I have been able to sound reasonably coherent in this description of my earlier failures, which makes me realise that despite them I have become more healthy. I think my determination was more important than the faith I placed in other people.

Summary

In this last section I want to summarise why my experiences were 'failures' and what might have been therapeutic.

I feel a little uneasy in attributing so much of the blame to Dr Parker and Mary, rather than considering my part in the difficulties. But then again, *I* was the client, so of course I was disturbed! In fact, with Mary, I felt that I *did* try quite hard to make allowances for her, and even with Dr Parker I kept coming back until *he* gave up.

I have mentioned the coldness and unresponsiveness of Dr Parker as contributing to the failure. I know that in his approach he would want to portray a 'blank screen' on to which I would imagine all sorts of things. I have thought about this a lot, and I really believe that by being unresponsive he was actually displaying quite a lot on to that screen. In our culture, a person who displays unresponsiveness in the face of such desperation and need is portraying a clear picture of being 'uncaring' or even 'cruel'.

I have spoken about Mary's nervousness and warmth, that felt skin deep, as contributors to our failure. But as I piece together this summary I realise that there was one thing in common between Mary and Dr Parker that really feels at the kernel of the difficulty I had with both of them as helpers: they were both *inflexible* people. It felt that Dr Parker had his way of relating with clients that he would use regardless of the client and the way he or she behaved. Mary was also inflexible in the sense that she could not 'let go' and just be natural. Her defensiveness, and perhaps her moralistic values, meant that we had to walk a narrow track rather than a broad path together.

In looking at what might have been therapeutic for me in a counsellor, I am surprised to realise that I really did not need a lot in either case. I needed to feel *warmth* and a sense of *commitment*. In the first failure I also needed someone who would be prepared to *hold* me, not necessarily physically, though that would have helped. More than that, in both cases, I needed someone who was so *secure* in themselves that they could reach out to *me* — a person who was insane.

3 A Client's Experience of Success

Myra Grierson

Psychiatry before Counselling

The beginning was deep depression, shutting myself down. Neither eating nor speaking. Being still, curled up, removed from life. The process prior to 'talking' therapy was full of peaks and troughs. There are vague recollections and vivid incidents intermingled with nameless faces and places without identity. The doctors spoke but I cannot recall their words. I was given drug therapy and Electro-Convulsive Therapy (ECT). I do not remember agreeing to this treatment and nothing was explained. I do not recall being asked. I do not remember telling my story or of being listened to by anyone. What I do remember was a feeling of being judged to be weak and without value either to myself or others.

> Once,
> there was nothing I would
> dare to want.

> Once,
> there was nothing I
> deserved.

> Once,
> was long ago.
> Now,
> I can have everything . . .

There was a time when being linked to success in counselling was beyond my comprehension. The possibility that someone, some-where, might actually listen to me, ask me to tell them my story and accept me was not even considered. I did not know that I needed a listener, a companion in my pain. All I knew in that far-off time was a need to go back to some forgotten safe place which I sensed had once existed but had no tangible substance that I could identify. At first I tried to reach it by withdrawing from the world physically and emotionally. I gave up speech and nourishment. I shadowed on the edge of the deep pit of black despair which threatened to swallow me. I flirted with that dark place which vibrated with messages, promises of oblivion and an ending to my pain. I tried to kill myself but discovered that although I had the enthusiasm for suicide, or so it seemed, I did not have the total commitment, nor the means.

My life was a nightmare of numbness, occasionally punctuated by personal loss, depression, hospitalisation and a deep sense of being lost and of isolation. I fitted in nowhere and found it hard to live in the world. I make these statements in retrospect because the 'me' in that time and place was unable to articulate her needs, and she was certainly without either self-esteem or personal insight. I was emotionally and physically immature. I floundered in a sea of hard edges and deep places. I managed to float for most of the time but there was always the treacherous wave which periodically engulfed me, though I never quite drowned.

The First Experience of Counselling

By the time I was offered 'talking' therapy I was nearing a decade of drugs and the occasional appointment with a psychiatrist for ten minutes at a busy out-patient clinic. Once I was asked if I minded a student sitting in on my session — I was discussed as if I had suddenly become invisible. I remember my anger as I heard the details. Was I so stupid that I could not be trusted to understand my own illness? Could no one see my need to know? Another doctor stated that 'Women of your class have to be content with what they have.' However, that dismissive value judgement was surpassed by a later doctor, whose reaction to my grief at the end of my marriage was to say: 'What you need in your life are a few more children — then you wouldn't have time to feel sorry for yourself.'! My anger, desolation and grief were overwhelming.

I had learned about group counselling through a television programme and began to make enquiries about this possibility. I have no memory of how I came to hear about the group I applied to join. I had been admitted to hospital again and went off to see the doctor who was running the group at a nearby city psychiatric clinic. I remember the fear I felt when I saw the doctor was a woman. My relationships with women were very bad at this time. She told me that I could not join the group because I was a patient in hospital once again. I was deeply shocked at her words; she was telling me I was ineligible, I was not 'well enough'. I remember feeling numb and full of despair. How 'well' had I to be before I was given help? I felt a sense of hopelessness about the whole set-up of care and treatment for people like me. There seemed nowhere to go, nowhere to take my suffering, nowhere to be heard. The following week I was offered the chance to be treated in a different way. It was not named as such but it was counselling.

I remember my fear and felt that in a sense it was unreal. Were they really telling me I could talk to this man across the desk from me? I was scared that it might be just another attempt by them to make me 'pull myself together'. However, it was genuine and he was quite open about his offer to me from the beginning. He was a doctor who was undertaking training as a counsellor and I was to be one of his 'practice' clients. I felt very impressed at the time by his openness; he honestly valued me and I sensed he really cared. That was the beginning of the long journey to find my 'self'.

The process was very straightforward as far as I could observe. I talked and talked and he listened in an active way which was very important for me. It seemed to spill out, nothing chronologically, nothing in its place, just a gigantic story of suffering and loss. My life — or as much of it as I was prepared to share with him at the time — was spread between us like some ragged patchwork quilt that was full of holes and very thin in places. My driving force was that I needed to work, to catch up on all those twilight years and he was simply a tool to facilitate my recovery. I felt a surge of hope for the first time. Looking back, I see it as being the end of the abuse that had been heaped upon me in the guise of 'treatment' and the beginning of my finding my voice, and taking responsibility for my own life.

I am conscious now of how powerful I saw the counsellor. I felt that he was the final authority on most of the events that were taking place in my life at that time. I was also rather mixed up about what was supposed to be happening in the relationship between us. There was no contract or discussion about what was appropriate during these meetings and no money was involved. My rights in the relationship were not discussed and no time was specified for each session nor how many sessions I could expect to have. It was scary and I felt uncertain about the future commitment of the counsellor. I know now that I was just too scared to ask these questions in case he stopped seeing me. I might have been rejected again. Though the experience was good, my defences were limitless and I became quite skilled in avoiding areas which were unsafe for me in the interaction between us. An example of this was my inability to deal with another person's anger in relation to me, and it was unthinkable to be angry with him. He might have responded angrily in return and that thought was quite frightening.

At the beginning I saw him for two or three sessions each week but later the pace of our work together slowed down and I began to see him only once. I had been discharged from hospital by this time and gradually began to feel, look and behave differently. I took charge of my life and enrolled at a local college of further education. I made new friends and related with them differently: for example, I began to be less threatened by women and actually developed a deep friendship with a woman which has been very good for me and continues to grow in strength. My fear of commitment to others also dissipated. My ability as a mother improved and I began to plan my future for the first time in my life.

My counsellor was always available and I saw him intermittently over the next three years. I do not think I ever abused this accessibility, and its safety often meant that I did not actually need to meet or talk to him in order to deal with any problems I had.

When I review my time with him I can focus on those events within the therapeutic relationship which produced change in me. The most important was my perception of him as an ordinary person like myself. This happened in a dramatic way, one day, half-way through a session. I had been seeing him for about four months and our sessions had developed into an easy pattern of my dealing with the feelings that had arisen for me in the preceding interval. That day, as we worked, I heard footsteps outside the door and a key turned in the lock. A nurse, not aware that there was someone in the room, had locked the door. My counsellor suddenly realised what was happening and jumped up with fear and panic on his face. I remember feeling disbelief at his reaction and anger too that he did not trust me to be alone with him in a locked room. I knew all the rational reasons why it might be unsafe for him but I felt very uncomfortable abut his reaction. I confronted him with my feelings, expressed my displeasure at his apparent lack of confidence in me and then I saw him as he really was — a man who was better educated than me but as frail and as human as myself. This observation marked an important shift in our relationship. I knew that I had to be responsible for myself now; I was the one who had to do the work. I was the only one who could change my life. That shift for me was about power. I felt for the first time that he was as powerful as I allowed him to be in the relationship. The balance prior to this had all been tilted towards him. Before this incident I felt that if I was not a 'good' patient perhaps he would get fed up and the sessions would stop. If I let him see too much of my 'bad self' he might not value me at all. It had been difficult for me to understand that being vulnerable was what counselling was all about.

When I met this counsellor recently he revealed that he had experienced me as treating him as a parental figure. There had been no real discussion between us about this aspect of our relationship at the time it was happening. However, he did once ask me if I knew what 'transference' was and although I said 'Yes', my understanding was very hazy.

His willingness to help me recognise my ability to do more with my life was very important to my self-esteem. He arranged for me to see a psychologist who tested my cognitive ability. The good results of the testing gave me the incentive to begin studying at a higher level and to make long-term plans for my future education and career. Within the space of six years I went from being unable to put two words together (because of the enduring effects of ECT) to graduating from university.

The initial relationship with this counsellor lasted for two to three years with occasional meetings over the next decade. I knew, and hoped, there was always someone there. Our sessions together were intermittent and often too far apart for anything therapeutic to take place. I never really worked through any new material in those years of sparse contact. I often felt that I needed more time than he gave. In the latter stages our sessions of twenty to thirty minutes were not long enough to go deeply into anything and each time my emotions and circumstances were different. I did not know how to ask for what I needed because I was unsure of what my rights as a client were and I was afraid he might become angry and reject me. I know he was, and still is, my friend and I am certain that he saved my life.

I had sorted through many of the problems in my life and I had become much more self-aware. However, in retrospect, I was merely acquiring a new set of defence mechanisms to ward off the problems I had in relating to other people. I was able to cope reasonably well with my life but there was always a residue of unfinished business shadowing on the edge of my awareness. I often experienced dissatisfaction with the way I was relating to my family and friends. There was a feeling of unhappiness and a sense of being 'stuck' in a pattern of behaviour which was somehow destructive. In effect, I had only scraped the surface and papered over the cracks. I was unaware, however, of what was happening to me. I had exchanged the parenting of my counsellor for that of a new marriage and my life was relatively stable and happy. It was hard to trust my feelings while I slowly edged my way through career and personal relationships, keeping as safe as I could, and I was always aware that my self-destruction was only pushed away and not fully resolved. I had done enough in that first therapeutic relationship to become a person who seemed strong and able to overcome those obstacles that arose from time to time in her life. I was okay . . .

The Second Experience of Counselling

What I brought to the next counselling relationship that I embarked upon, and which has continued for the past three-and-a-half years, was what I thought to be an integrated person. I presented this seemingly good-natured being who was always ready to please — too ready. I would give of my time and energy to whoever needed it, but I was full of self-doubt, unresolved anger and grief, well concealed under a layer of defensive behaviour patterns which served me well. I needed to be liked and I used my sense of humour by always laughing and joking, to keep those people in my immediate social circle pleased and seeming to like me.

Whereas the previous counselling relationship had begun with my feeling very helpless and powerless to make choices about what might happen, this one began as a conscious act, with the counsellor and I forming a contract. It involved a financial agreement which was to last over a long period and negotiations about when and where we were to meet as well as the length of each session. Once that was agreed we moved on to discuss other elements of our 'understanding'. I spoke about how crucial it was for me to feel safe with him: if I did not trust his acceptance of me then I could not speak openly. He acknowledged that there would undoubtedly be times when I did not want to disclose.

This helped me to realise that I had *choices* in as much as I could decide what was safe for me to disclose of myself at any given time. He, by his acknowledgement of my 'secret' places, helped me to feel a sense of acceptance from him which encouraged me to trust him. I felt that he knew I was not all sweetness and light but that he respected the timing of how much I could reveal of myself and how vulnerable I could allow myself to be in relation to him. It seems now, when I look back at this beginning of our work together, that what I felt was a great deal of uncertainty. I was not sure of his commitment at that time but the process of establishing the working contract helped me to feel reasonably safe. I was able to say to him, 'I'm so scared' and it was not dismissed in any way. I was *actively* listened to and my feelings were acknowledged — for instance, he said: 'You seem very unsure of what you can risk with me.' When I acknowledged that my fear was a normal reaction to the newness of the relationship and that it was accepted by him I began to feel much safer and more comfortable. I wrote the following early in our relationship:

> I know I am the client in this relationship with this man who listens to my story. I know that our contract has been set down and that I have choices

in these meetings between us but, can I really *trust* that? Can I really trust that he will not judge me or disapprove of me? Will he be *strong* enough to listen to the pain of it all? Can I really be me in the relationship?

When I open up to him will he step back from me and not want to know me? I feel such a sense of fear that I will be rejected. I want to know him but he does not seem to give of himself in the way that I need and that scares me a lot. Does he see me as some sort of a wimp who cannot get it together — someone who is just inadequate and weak? It is often very hard for me to go and sit opposite this person from whom I need too much for my own good. Sometimes I wonder what on earth he does this work for — what is his angle — what's in it for him?

I often feel quite suspicious of him and when I take risks I feel helpless and vulnerable after I leave him and remember what I have let him see of me. Often I experience great periods of chaos and uncertainty after our session together. What really scares me, of course, is the possibility that he will decide that he does not want to be in this relationship with me — that feels very scary. I try hard to guard against trying to please him by being an 'interesting client'. There are often times when I feel I am boring him but I am too scared to say that because he might say 'Yes', and reject me as his client.

I feel that if he sees I am working hard and taking risks then he will experience my commitment and value my effort. Sometimes I am so eager to work that I cannot wait for him. I rush on, ever aware of the time and of my need to communicate. I feel myself bombarding him with sound and his acceptance of that is very important to me in our relationship.

My Power/His Acceptance

Power was a new word for me to use in relation to myself. Here I was in a relationship with a counsellor who was offering me the opportunity not only to explore my power but actually to use it outside of our sessions. I remember my feelings of disbelief as I became aware of my power as a client. Was this man really taking this shit from me; this telling of my story, over and over again? I worked almost frantically in an effort to get it all out before he said 'Let's stop now', at the end of each session. It took me a long time to hear these straightforward words without experiencing the feeling of rejection. It was as if he were saying, 'Go away. I do not want to be with you any more.' I began to experience myself as being afraid of him. I needed him to give me his attention and time. My neediness exposed me to a great wave of vulnerability. Did he really accept my way of trying to get what I needed from him? Since I did not accept my own behaviour I did not trust this man who *seemed* to be accepting me without question. When this trust eventually came, the feeling of being accepted was very powerful. I was on a train, going over a previous session in my mind, when the realisation came to me. The phrase 'too many words' kept popping into my head in an irritating kind of way which I could not shake off. Suddenly, I was consumed by a rush of emotion as I remembered my childhood with the repeated messages from my parents that I 'talked too much' and the feeling that they never listened to me. On the train I remembered these feelings of rejection and I wept noisily, ignoring the other passengers. I felt a mixture of anger and sadness. Anger towards the adults who had rejected me and deep sadness for the little girl I had been and who had tried to get the love she needed. Suddenly, I realised the extent of the care my counsellor had shown me. I felt very light and sort of free. I felt too a sense of awe as I understood the significance of this shift. He had been able to stay with me and accept my torrent of words without being at all judgemental. He had done more for me than my family and they were supposed to be the ones who should have loved and cared. I felt very small and safe at that precise moment and I remember my face beaming with smiles as I got off the train. I was unaware of those around me and only now wonder if anyone noticed my behaviour. As a direct response to his caring of me, I began to be caring of him in return:

> I can see him try to stay with my stream of words. I feel such compassion for him. He is very gentle as he eases the pace into a lower gear and I know he values me. I feel understood and I trust him . . .

I felt as if I had been given a very valuable gift, which was the ability to see myself in a new way. I could feel my own value and I could value another in return.

His Style of Working

One of the most obvious aspects of my counsellor's way of working with me was his gentleness. His style was an even flow in the sense that he did not intrude in inappropriate ways. I felt no sense of him butting in whilst I was struggling to define or express my feelings. Often when I became distressed he seemed to be *actively* still; I could *feel* him being still. He never seemed jittery or anxious. Always, I had a sense of him being prepared to meet me on an emotional level. I experienced him as being centred.

His actual physical presence was very much part of his style. In appearance he looked solid and strong. His actions were unhurried and he displayed a calm, even temper, touched with just the correct level of humour, to which I responded warmly. However, sometimes this sense of his strength and stability was rather intimidating for me because it was hard for me to see his vulnerability. I was not sure how he received mine. Was he judging me to be weak and ineffectual? For a long time I was wary of this aspect of our relationship and it was not until we reached a crisis point that I felt it was resolved. I saw his continual acceptance of me as incongruent. His calmness, I felt, was often a cover-up for the boredom he was experiencing as I seemed to be going over old ground and feeling quite stuck. I challenged him with a sense of fear which left me feeling shaky: 'I feel I'm boring you and yet you go on listening and we don't talk about the boredom. . . . I feel you're not open with me. . . .' It was such a relief when he said: 'Yes, it has often felt boring. . . . You going over the same stuff. . . . I got really fed up sometimes. . . .' I am sure that if he had denied or rejected my feelings the relationship would have ended then. What happened instead was that I became able to use our relationship to realise things about myself.

Trusting his honesty, I asked him to say more on how he saw me. One of the things he said was that throughout our long contact he had never perceived me as a *sexual* person. After this he said:

> *Him*: I feel like I've taken a huge risk telling you that. . . . I don't know what that's about for me.
> *Me*: For me it's about being here in this relationship with you as a *child*. . . . I've never been grown up here! . . . I've never felt as if I've related to you sexually. I've been too little. . . .

This session was a crucial part of our work together for many reasons. It was important for me to see him being 'vulnerable' in speaking of his boredom and in his uncertainty and discomfort over giving me his perceptions of my sexuality. It was also useful to identify my childlike way of being with him. Of course that led to me becoming more 'adult', while he became less gentle and more confronting. This led the relationship to a more realistic position. I could feel a sense of shared power. I was able to take more risks and test out my own power in a way which left me vulnerable *but* essentially safe. I felt that I could be more open about my negative feelings and trust that I would be understood and not judged. I felt now we were working together more in the moment. In retrospect, I wish he had been more challenging and that I had experienced him taking more risks earlier, but, at the same time, I had felt safe with his valuing of my pace. I never felt he had an agenda for me and the timing of the work had seemed under my guidance. His ability to accompany me and to accept me exactly where I was had meant that I was always aware of his valuing and respect of me as a person. I can see that his style is totally geared to the pace of the client and I feel that by working at a slow pace I was able to experience my shifts at a level which led to a more effective way of relating.

Anger

I think that of all the feelings I experienced in relation to this man, anger was the most empowering. At first I was aware of it as merely irritation, a feeling of discontent with what I saw as his incongruence in our sessions together. I did not believe his apparent acceptance of me. I felt I was boring him and I wanted him to acknowledge that fact. His sitting there, session after session, accepting whatever I produced seemed totally wrong. I became aggressive and truculent, finding fault with him in my mind. My anger began to surface but I could not deal with it during our sessions. I felt I was becoming an ugly, bitchy person as I began to see his faults and I was not sure that he was working to maintain our relationship. My internal struggle was about my fear of anger in others and my inability to be angry in a constructive way. For instance, in the past my anger had been about my losing control, going mad, shouting and throwing things. I was also scared of other people's anger and avoided that at all costs. Now, I was in a situation where I was getting angrier and angrier with my counsellor. The implications of this plunged me into a state of alarm because of possible rejection by him. Eventually, the feeling leaked out and I knew I could not go on holding it down. I said to myself, 'Fuck it. In for a penny, in for a pound.' I remember my feelings as I sat opposite him on the day I had decided to tell him how angry I was. The first words I blurted out were: 'I am really angry. . . . You do not seem to give me anything of yourself. . . . I don't know you. I don't know who you are and that pisses me off!' I felt as if I had dropped a bomb into the middle of the room. I was aware of my anger falling away from me as he responded by saying: 'Yes, that's right. I haven't always been open with you. . . . I can see you are angry with me.' I realised suddenly that he was not going to be angry in response but that he was prepared to discuss the reason for my anger. He did not throw me out — he did not reject me. Instead, it was as if he was prepared to fight for what we had in the relationship. I began to sense my own value and with it came a rising level of self-esteem. I had been ugly, bitchy and boring with him and yet he was willing to continue with the contract. I was able to talk about what I saw as the unacceptable part of my personality and to say, 'But I am also loving, caring, sensitive, intuitive, creative, sexual and lovable.' I felt at last the continuous presence of my 'self'. I was no longer disjointed and all over the place. I was real — the mask was slipping away.

Being Understood
I know that one of the major realisations to surface in relation to my counsellor was that my darkest feelings were acknowledged and accepted by him. This happened when I was experiencing a period of acute distress in my personal life. I felt again that old feeling of

wanting to die, accompanied by a sense of despair and calm resignation. 'I just feel I want to die . . . end it all . . . kill myself. I'm just too tired. I don't want to live anymore. I'm tired of the struggle. . . .' I noticed he became very still and he spoke very gently and quietly: 'Your life seems very painful . . . you feel as if you can't go on. . . . I feel you've taken a big risk telling me that. . . .' Almost at once I felt a wave of relief. He was not going to talk me out of the feeling or get me to see that my life was worth living. I felt he did not want to exert control over my actions. I experienced my feelings being respected at a deep level. I felt as if a heavy burden was falling away from me and I relaxed and experienced a sense of lightness. Even the room seemed to become brighter.

I am certain that his helping me to stay with what I was feeling made the sense of shame and guilt, which always seemed to accompany my feelings of wanting to die, gradually ease away. I realised also that he was not afraid to go with me into the blackness of my internal confusion. I felt he understood my distress and accepted the reality of my inner world. I had communicated how I felt — I was aware of being completely understandable.

From that moment, I was able to realise and accept that this deep sense of self-destruction was just as much part of me as any of what I perceived as the 'positive bits' of my personality.

The shift that came later that week was very sudden and totally unexpected. I was shopping in a local supermarket and I saw someone trying to control one of those rogue trollies that seem always to jump out at you when you are in a hurry. Quite suddenly the word *control* came into my mind. I realised then that by killing my 'self' I would be exercising the ultimate control. It had seemed to be the only real control in my life for many years. If my world did not give me what I needed then I could remove myself from it. The logical normality of this struck me and I knew that I had never been 'mad' or 'crazy' but paradoxically both powerful and powerless at the same time. I could not control the events in my life at that time but I could control what I did with my 'self'.

I know that I might experience that feeling of wanting to die again in the future but I am not afraid of it or ashamed of it any more. I was able through my relationship with this man to give meaning to what was a potentially dangerous feeling. I know too that it is a signal from deep inside myself telling me to pay attention to my needs and to accept and care for myself.

Conclusion

The way I experienced 'change' in counselling seems important. All the things I discovered came at my pace and from my frame of reference. As each new shift was internalised I could sense a pattern developing. Feeling myself moving towards some unknown insight meant that I began to experience great faith in my ability to take power over my life and change my ways of relating. The most important fact was that it came from *within me* and I was free to choose how and when I used my change.

Looking back now, I can see that I was able to incorporate, very gradually, new ways of being my self. Instead of struggling just to cope with my life I experienced my self being brave and not being scared to take risks with my personal relationships. I was able to be clearer in my mind about what I needed in my life and to use that clarity to help me get it. I stopped being manipulative and could ask for what I needed. Last week I said to my counsellor: 'I need you to love and care for me. . . .' That was an alarming intimacy for me but he smiled in a warm way and I felt that warmth touch me in some deep place. I found myself smiling, glad that I had taken such a risk. The pay-off was that I could be loving and accepting of myself now.

In retrospect I can see that both of these relationships had much in common but there was also a marked difference between them. The most obvious contrast for me was the setting up of the contract in the second experience. That initial exploration of what the process was and what my rights were in the relationship gave me a feeling of safety which ultimately led me to experience my power in relation to this person. I can recognise also that the first relationship was less safe because I was the *chosen* and not the *chooser*. In the second instance, the fact that I was consciously seeking counselling meant I had already begun the process for myself — I was committed to the work ahead and I understood what was on offer. The most obvious similarity between the two experiences was the level of care that I felt from both counsellors. I experienced them both as very caring and respectful of me as a person. They were both prepared to offer encouragement beyond the counselling session and that helped me to experience my own value. Recently I asked my first counsellor about his action in helping me realise that I had the potential to study at a higher level in spite of the enormous problems I experienced with the residual effects of the ECT. He said that he referred me on to the psychologist in a gesture of friendship rather than through any feeling he had of intervention. The fact that he was able to remember that incident so clearly helped me to realise that I was not just a patient but a real person.

Being in a therapeutic relationship is both powerful and frightening. It is also rewarding and exciting. There were times in the past when the chaos I felt made me want to stop and give up. However, I have come to value my chaos because it is a sign that there is something going on inside me which will eventually sort itself out and I will move towards a new clarity. It was often a great effort to get myself to the sessions when I felt confused and scared. But gradually I found that I could both accept that fear and even work with it to great effect in our sessions.

Finally, one of the most delicious things that has happened to me as a result of counselling is a blossoming of my creativity, which I never dreamed existed. The world has become more exciting and I feel like an adventurer reaching out to discover newness. My change is not some invisible thing which cannot be checked out. I can see it, feel it and communicate it to others. I feel more loving and caring. In return, I receive more love and care from others.

I feel successful, I am successful and I know I will go on succeeding in my effort to become a whole person. I feel a great sense of being centred in my way of being me!

4 The Experience of Couple Counselling

Paul and Rosanne

Introduction by Paul

Two years ago Rosanne and I approached a counsellor we shall call Joe because we were experiencing difficulties in our relationship. We had been partners for about two years, were living together without being married and Rosanne was pregnant. It was a planned pregnancy and we were both committed to our relationship. However, the tensions and conflicts we were experiencing were causing both of us much anguish and we knew we needed professional help.

Our backgrounds were in many respects quite different. Rosanne had been married before and had a twelve-year-old daughter called Mary who was living with us. Rosanne's parents divorced when she was very young. She had little contact with her father and experienced her mother as depriving and sometimes abandoning. I had not been married and had not had much experience in sexual relationships. Aged thirty-one, I am six years younger than Rosanne. I grew up in an outwardly stable middle-class family, but one which was stifling and suffocating, creating conflicts for me as I tried to live my own separate independent life. Both Rosanne and I were training as psychotherapists and were on the same course. This was where we had met. We share many interests and views about political and social issues and both of us have backgrounds of working in childcare — Rosanne as a teacher and myself as a social worker.

It was quite easy to choose a counsellor. We both knew Joe as a tutor on our training course and had read and liked the books he had written. Rosanne particularly liked his understanding of feminist issues, and we both felt respect for him, valuing his style and approach in humanistic counselling. We were looking for fairly short-term counselling because both of us were already in individual therapy and we knew we could not afford to pay for both over a long period. We also predicted that it might be difficult to combine couple counselling and individual therapy in the long term.

There were a number of difficulties we were experiencing. First, we had sexual problems which seemed to be getting worse; secondly, we disagreed about how to parent Mary; thirdly, there were conflicts over boundaries which left me feeling restricted and invaded and left Rosanne feeling angry and deprived of intimacy; and fourthly, we had arguments that were mutually accusing and sometimes hysterical — very occasionally these escalated into minor violence involving slaps or hair-pulling. These difficulties reached a point of crisis on the weekend before we sought help from Joe. During this weekend I had reached the end of my tether and walked out on the Saturday night. I did not know where I was going but eventually stayed overnight with my older sister, and did not telephone Rosanne to let her know where I was until late the following morning. Later I regretted this when I discovered the degree of anxiety Rosanne had experienced during the night, and considered the possible damage such stress can cause to an unborn baby. She was three months' pregnant at this time and we agreed that we could not go on as we were. We had to seek help in the form of couple counselling.

In the pages that follow we try to describe our experiences of the couple counselling which took place over three months, during which time we usually had a weekly session lasting one hour in Joe's home. It is now twenty-one months since we ended our couple counselling and some of the intensity of the experience has faded, but we try to recapture it and put it into words under four main headings. There is the *symbolic* work where we were using symbols to explore the conflicts between us. There are the *themes* that emerged from the symbolic work, and from the counselling process as we went further into it. There is the *pattern* of the counselling, which seems important to include because at times we both felt that couple counselling made us feel even more despairing than we had done before. There is the *ending* and some reflections on the after-effects of the counselling. In these sections each of us tries to describe our own individual experience, so that there will often be two different views of what was happening, sometimes complementary views, sometimes conflicting. Before describing the symbolic work, Rosanne writes about how it felt to begin.

How it Felt to Begin, by Rosanne

Joe had set out two large armchairs for us in his small consulting room and I remember going in nervously and wondering where to sit. I thought the room had a friendly atmosphere. However, I felt vulnerable and aware of being pregnant. I really did not know what to expect — although I was used to individual psychotherapy this situation made me feel much more exposed. I hung back and let Paul speak first and then felt angry because he told Joe about our conflicts without mentioning my pregnancy at all. I think I hung back so much because of my anxiety about turns — would it be fair, would we take turns to speak to Joe? I did not want to push in and appear competitive, and also I wanted to see if Joe would take care of me by giving me my turn. I was relieved when he did and turned towards me to hear my account of the problems between Paul and myself. I also felt like I wanted to run away and not admit how sad I felt about our relationship, and how guilty that I was pregnant amidst such a furore. I expected disapproval, (though I knew rationally that no counsellor would show such a lack of understanding), and my own voice was shaky and unsure when I spoke.

One of the frightening aspects for me about beginning couple counselling was the lack of control. I was not in control of what was revealed by Paul, and it reminded me of being a little girl and wanting my friends, brothers and sisters not to 'tell tales on me'. Behind all this was a desire to be understood and to be taken seriously. In connection with this I was afraid that the two men would ally against me because they were both male and so I would be 'left out'. The first session helped me feel more secure. Paul and Joe did not join forces against me and there was some relief in just talking about our difficulties.

Joe seemed warm towards me and fair. I did not even want to leave at the end of the session as he seemed to provide a haven for both Paul and myself.

Symbolic Work

The Black Knight and the Water, by Rosanne

During an early session, Joe asked us to imagine something that would represent what we were each feeling. The symbol that emerged for Paul was a black knight, and though he was feeling strong, determined and confrontative he was not expecting such a warlike symbol. He liked the black knight as it seemed to represent an assertive part of himself. My symbol was water. I visualised a lake of peaceful water, quite deep and still. The knight frightened me. It was armoured and carrying a lance and I particularly disliked the rigidity. I remember how angry I felt that my beautiful water met with the knight.

Joe seemed to accept both symbols and later suggested that Paul stop giving me such a hard time, and that I needed to be prepared to fight back, rather than meeting his confrontations with a frustrating passivity. He suggested that Paul needed a more active response if he were not to feel as though he were thrashing around in the water. I felt angry about this and suspected that he was trying to persuade me to adapt to Paul's needs in a way which did not seem right to me. Paul, for his part, began to suspect that Joe was over-compensating for the fact that both he and Paul were men, by unfairly supporting me. For him, the advice not to give me such a hard time evoked these fears.

Through these symbols, a process was begun of discovering the true dynamic between Paul and myself at this time. It was like probing through layers of selfhood without really trying, as the symbols emerged easily and quickly. Events at home had been conflict-ridden. Seeing the black knight in my mind's eye made me realise that I did not want to surrender to Paul, yet the water was beckoning, mysterious and soft. It seemed we were locked in conflict. Joe drew our attention to a general imbalance of energies in our relationship whereby Paul was being very actively masculine, and I was being very receptively feminine. Both of us realised that we needed to balance the energies inside ourselves and in our relationship. An additional complexity which Joe perceived was that I was more assertive in the world outside the home than within our relationship. For Paul, the reverse was true. Paul also felt perplexed and irritated because Joe's insight did not seem to fit in with what he had explored in his own individual therapy. Joe was perceiving him as over-assertive, whereas his individual therapist was encouraging him to express himself more assertively. Initially he felt torn between the two insights but this difficulty was overcome when he realised that at different times and in different places he would swing between the two extremes of behaviour.

The Witch and the Librarian/Policeman, by Rosanne
During another session Joe asked us each to allow a symbol to emerge which would represent the other partner's most disliked qualities. Paul went first and came up with a witch as a symbol for me at the times he felt most negative about me. I was relieved because I feel quite positive about witches, but Paul expressed fear of the witch and wanted to keep her at a safe distance. The symbols that I imagined for Paul were, first, a librarian wearing glasses and a tie, and then an aggressive policeman in uniform with a hard hat and truncheon. I felt rebellious and angry with both of them and thought they disapproved of me and were withdrawn from me. I was afraid at the time that Paul really was the librarian and the policeman rolled into one, and that he would insist on rules and routines that

would stifle my spontaneity. Paul's wish to be more separate from me also aroused fears that he would want to be aloof and distant like the librarian and policeman. Later in the session Joe asked me if the symbols reminded me of anyone in my original family. I was surprised to find that they reminded me of my strict grandmother. Joe ventured an interpretation that she had been a 'phallic mother' figure, hard, rigid, unyielding and intrusive. I felt angry with him for this interpretation as I myself had not associated the male genital with my grandmother. I felt Joe himself was being intrusive at this point.

The powerful nature of the witch symbol prompted our counsellor to suggest that I needed to be more gentle with Paul. It might help if I were to imagine that he looked at me through a magnifying glass so that my actions appeared 'larger than life'. Then I felt exasperated with Joe because his observations were conflicting — he was telling me both that I needed to be more active and that I needed to be more gentle. I challenged this but Joe indicated that this was perfectly possible and held the contradictions for me in a way that I began to learn to do for myself.

Paul also experienced this session as difficult, and one in which he began to have some deeper and more intensely conflicting feelings about Joe. These surfaced when Joe pointed out that his symbol indicated that I needed to treat him gently because within him was a fragile, frightened little child-part. On the one hand he welcomed Joe's recognition of his difficulties and fears, feeling that Joe saw him more clearly and that the image of the black knight was now balanced by the image of a frightened little boy facing a witch. On the other hand, he felt that by focussing on this aspect of him Joe was belittling him and unfairly placing responsibility upon him for the difficulties which he and I were encountering. He felt this particularly when Joe suggested that he probably needed to regress to some early level of experience in his own individual therapy. Paul felt angry with Joe though he did not express this, perhaps because of a general difficulty he experiences in expressing feelings of anger towards male authority figures whose opinions he generally respects.

At one point in the session Joe asked Paul if the witch reminded him of anyone else. Paul replied that it reminded him of his older sister Stephanie, who was the most independent, rebellious and strong-willed child in his original family. He also said that the witch reminded him of his grandmother who complained a great deal. Focussing his attention in this way helped Paul to become more aware of the qualities in me that both attracted and repelled him, and of the influence which his childhood experience of his grandmother and sister had upon his current relationship with me.

The Little Devil and the Heart, by Paul
At the beginning of one of the middle sessions I began telling Joe
about the struggles I was having with Rosanne's daughter, Mary,
when I tried to set limits on her behaviour. I felt that Rosanne did
not support me adequately and allowed Mary to play us off against
each other. I described Mary as behaving omnipotently, at which
point Joe confronted me on this issue by asking me about my own
omnipotence. I struggled, feeling rather powerless, to answer the
question by agreeing that I sometimes behaved omnipotently. Joe
then asked me whether any symbol came to mind when I thought
about Mary. Immediately I imagined a little black devil figure. I was
rather taken aback by the nature and clear association of this
symbol. Rosanne for her part felt very angry with me for seeing
Mary as a devil. She had already experienced much disapproval
from her mother and sister about Mary's lack of 'manners' and free
way of expressing herself, and my criticisms seemed to be an
extension of her mother's disapproval.

The symbol representing Mary that came to mind for Rosanne
was that of a heart. Rosanne was surprised by this symbol because
it seemed 'too good', too 'lovey-dovey'. Intellectually she knew that
Mary was not perfect, and that their relationship was not all love,
but the emergence of the symbol of the heart helped her to see that
fundamentally she still idealised Mary, the two of them having been
very close after the breakup of Rosanne's marriage to Mary's
father.

Rosanne also thought that she saw surprise in Joe's facial
expression as he listened to the two symbols we had for Mary,
because they were so far apart. Certainly, for me, one of the
important insights which Joe gave us, arising out of this piece of
work, was that the imbalance of assertive active qualities and
passive receptive ones, which had emerged in the symbols of the
black knight and the water, was re-emerging in the way in which we
were perceiving Mary and were relating to her; for I was being very
assertively confrontative towards her, whereas Rosanne was being
very receptively nurturing and warm towards her. In the months
that followed, this insight helped us to correct the imbalance in our
ways of relating to Mary — for example, I would increasingly leave
space for Rosanne to be assertive with Mary rather than rush in to
be confrontative myself.

From our description of Mary's behaviour Joe also suggested that
she herself seemed to be splitting her view of Rosanne and myself
into 'good' mummy and 'bad' Paul, mirroring the rather split way in
which we seemed to be perceiving her. He thought that Mary was
old enough to be able to accept some insight from us on this matter,

letting her know what she was doing and confirming that there was both 'good' and 'bad' in both Rosanne and myself. When we shared this insight with Mary at a carefully chosen moment several months later, it seemed to strike a chord in her, and my impression was that she found it helpful.

Further Themes that Emerged

Sex, Anxiety and Responsibility, by Paul

Rosanne and I were experiencing sexual difficulties in our relationship at the time we approached Joe, and for one session we focussed exclusively upon this issue. I began describing the sexual difficulties I had encountered in past relationships, which included periodic impotence, years of abstinence and a general difficulty in experiencing a satisfying sexual orgasm. Initially Joe just listened attentively but eventually intervened and encouraged me to focus on our current sexual difficulties. Joe responded to our account of these difficulties sometimes by offering simple down-to-earth practical advice, which I experienced as helpful although Rosanne sometimes found it to be too technical. At other times Joe would encourage me in particular to accept more fully my own responsibility for my sexual experience. On one occasion he used a witty comment to get this point across to me. I had been describing my perception of Rosanne as being too passive to be exciting, and Joe replied 'Hey ho necrophilia here I come'. Rosanne appreciated the humour of this comment more fully than I did, and although I saw the point Joe was making I felt saddened that he was not really tuning into the despair I felt about my sexual experience.

During the weeks prior to seeking help from Joe I had been experiencing tension in my back, and feeling sick and unwell during and after sexual intercourse. Here Joe made a simple link between this sensation and the fact that Rosanne's pregnancy was leading me to feel worried and anxious about the additional responsibilities, emotional and financial, which I would experience following the birth of our child. This insight helped me to feel understood, as well as providing a great deal of relief for Rosanne as it confirmed that it was my own anxieties, and not anything that she was doing, that was causing me to feel sick.

In some respects both of us, though Rosanne to a greater extent than I, felt some dissatisfaction that in discussing our sexual difficulties, we had not probed very deeply. It was perhaps the least resolved area in the couple counselling. Nonetheless, it produced a lessening of tension, which enabled both of us to experience less anxiety on account of our sexual difficulties, and gradually, though with many ups and downs, our mutual sexual satisfaction has been enhanced. Furthermore, we have generally been able to talk about our sexual relationship with less recourse to unhelpful, acrimonious accusations.

Abandonment and Suffocation, by Rosanne

During counselling it emerged that Paul and I had two childhood experiences that were opposite in kind and were easily re-stimulated by each other's behaviour. For me it was abandonment that brought anguish which I sought either to avoid, or to precipitate, in order to 'get it over with'. For Paul, suffocation was the great threat, and he felt he had to shut me out in order to feel free. This became very clear when we did an exercise at Joe's suggestion in which we stood up with a distance of a few feet between us, and then one of us stayed still while the other was instructed to advance as close to the other as was felt to be 'comfortable'. I was the one who wanted to move close and would have liked to finish in each other's arms. Paul recognised during the couple counselling that his need to pull away from me often caused me to feel that he had abandoned me. Joe advised him to pull away when he felt the urge, but to approach me again as soon as he felt he could.

The Inner Children, by Rosanne

I became aware during the couple counselling of what felt like a child inside me, by which I mean not the baby in my womb, but a part of myself which was entirely made up of the residue of childhood experiences. This inner child was very vulnerable, afraid of abandonment and afraid of anger. I found Joe a good father to my inner child. He supported the most fragile part of me, particularly in relation to Paul's rage. This was a strong rage which Paul dealt with by shouting and hitting cushions. Unfortunately, sometimes the cushions were very near me and I experienced anxiety and frightened feelings of my own when this happened. I recall Joe suggesting that Paul hit the cushions in another room instead of near me. I felt much safer when Paul followed this advice, though I hasten to add that it was actually me who was occasionally violent to the extent of hitting out one or two times in despair. I had not known any close relationship totally devoid of violence before and I found it hard to imagine that a relationship could be free from such physical aggression.

My experience in couple counselling was sometimes that of being perfectly understood by the counsellor. This experience was so healing that I suspect it is the basis of successful counselling. When my fear of Paul's rage was understood it gave me renewed strength.

Another time this happened was when I desperately wanted Paul to touch my belly in which our baby was developing. I did not even have to express this to Joe who asked Paul right away whether he had as yet touched the baby. He recommended that he do so as soon as possible, saying it would be good for all of us. Here again the needs of my inner child were understood.

Paul became aware of his inner child too, and discovered how easily he lost his awareness of this part of himself in his day-to-day relationship with me. This was most evident in the sessions where we explored the symbols of the witch and the librarian/policeman when he became aware of the frightened little boy inside him facing a witch.

Trust, Power and Anger, by Rosanne

During the time in counselling we continued to express anger to each other in great rows that left us exhausted and deeply wounded. I felt guilty after such rows and describing them to the counsellor I found myself expecting disapproval. However, he accepted our descriptions without judgement and suggested that we try to follow a code when arguing. This code consisted of a few simple rules — you do not shout, accuse, ask questions which are really statements, swear, label, blame, hit or psychologise the other person. You also do not exaggerate. I found the code very difficult to practise and realise that it calls for great balance and self-control at a time when I feel least rational. I did not like the code because I felt doomed to fail in practising it, and because it was something imposed from the outside to modify my behaviour, while it could not help me with the feelings I had inside.

Paul liked the code and thought it very useful, and he was at times able to practise it. He felt safer having ground rules even if they were not entirely attainable. He felt grateful to the counsellor for suggesting them, whereas I felt resentful, though my general feelings of warmth towards Joe were not undermined.

Pattern of the Counselling, by Paul

As we looked back on our couple counselling it seemed to both Rosanne and myself that there were four distinct phases in it. First, there was an *opening* period when, as we explored our relationship, we seemed to experience some improvements in it as well as a growing understanding. There then followed a second period when our relationship seemed to deteriorate, hitting *rock bottom* in one session where feelings of intensified distrust and paranoia were emerging and being expressed. In particular, I recall fearing that Rosanne was trying to turn my family and friends against me, and I insisted that she did not contact one of my sisters without first telling me. As Joe listened to my account, which I have only briefly sketched here, and my unwillingness to hear his suggestion that my demands in this respect were unreasonable, he seemed to be in despair himself and said that my account seemed like madness. I was rather shaken by this comment, and remember discussing its implications anxiously in my next individual therapy session. Rosanne and I had indeed reached rock bottom in our relationship and I felt that I had reached rock bottom in exploring myself. There seemed nowhere else to go but upwards and somehow, having centred ourselves, we approached the next session quite differently, looking for ways forwards to heal ourselves and our relationship.

It seemed to me that Joe intuitively recognised this change in our approach soon after the beginning of the session and helped us into the third phase, which we call *resurfacing*, by asking us to do an exercise. In this exercise he asked each of us to imagine inviting the other 'into the deepest place I know within myself' and asked us to consider what we would say to the other who had been invited into this place. We had to write our answer on a piece of paper simultaneously so that neither of us knew the other's reply until we had completed our own answer. My recollection of the exercise is that I wanted Rosanne to take care of such a place and to allow me to express myself freely. Rosanne's imagined response was to tell me that we would be warm and free in her deepest place. Joe suggested that these replies indicated a compatibility in us as partners perhaps because we both found it easy to invite the other into our 'deepest place' and that both of us valued the 'freedom' which would be there. In any case, Joe's observation confirmed for us that our relationship was worth the current struggle, that it could be more harmonious, and that we could meet each other's needs more easily. Hope had returned and we eventually moved on to the fourth stage — *ending*.

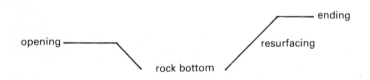

Figure 4.1   *The Four Phases of the Counselling*

An Abrupt Ending, by Rosanne

I was six-months' pregnant when we decided to stop our couple counselling, at least for a while. I was getting almost dangerously overtired because I was still working as well as training and the energy for counselling was lacking. I felt I needed more time to prepare emotionally and physically for the birth of our baby. We had a lot to integrate, as the work had been intense, and I suppose we had arrived at a point where it was clear that we had confronted the most difficult aspects of our relationship and opened up all the issues of which we were then aware. However, I recognise that we had only begun to find strengths and put the pieces back together again. We had continued the process down to 'rock bottom' and 'turned the corner', discovering through the exercise described in the last section that we did want to let each other into 'the deepest place I know'. More than ever, it seemed feasible to have such intimacy.

I felt we were deserting Joe when Paul told him that we were ending our couple counselling. It seemed unfair that we had not given him more warning, but just announced it abruptly. He took it with calmness and simply said he would be available if we needed him again. I greatly appreciated his flexibility — at no time had he tied us down to a complicated contract, but simply offered himself as a resource. Perhaps neither of us entirely wanted to let go of him, for we often thought of returning and it gave me a feeling of security to know that we could. However, nearly two years have now elapsed and we have not yet returned. I once took our baby boy to a place where I knew Joe would be, and I showed him our son. I felt self-conscious, as I knew I was trying to complete something.

Since the couple counselling we have never argued as destructively as before, though we do still argue of course. We rarely clash in parenting our son and get on very much better with Mary, but I believe there is a lot more to achieve sexually. The strength I experienced through couple counselling is the strength of facing 'the worst' together and surviving it, combined with the tremendous relief of being understood by the counsellor. Gradually I have come to see advantages in the almost opposite nature of our backgrounds. I benefit from the reliability and care that Paul's parents gave him, because they are somehow a part of him now. Perhaps he benefits from those aspects of my background that make it easier for me to break cultural norms (part of my witch), and from the respect for separateness and independence that existed in my original family despite the lack of care. I include these reflections because, although they emerged after we had stopped our couple counselling, I recognise that the experience continues as part of an inner process long after the sessions are ended.

5 The Client Becomes a Counsellor

Brendan McLoughlin

On Being a Client

I often feel I must have started life in search of meaning — at least that is the way it seems — and having been a client or a patient for over eight years, I now pursue that interest in meaning in my work as a counsellor.

Probably my very first 'therapy' experience was of an unwitting kind. I found myself in adolescence the author of a compulsive flow of poetry. Looking back I now recognise this as the spontaneous striving of my psyche to provide me with a container for my psychological distress. While these efforts clearly needed an interpreter, which they did not find, they are powerful reminders to me now, as a trained practitioner, of the self-assertive efforts of the psyche to express feelings and resolve conflicts. Years later I had the privilege of observing an infant grapple with experience from birth to two years old and I witnessed the same striving for resolution of indigestible bits of life. It has been important to me in becoming a counsellor to be sensitive to this 'striving' part of the client, allowing it enough space to guide the process along.

One of the poems I wrote as an adolescent said this:

four walls of yellow painted safety
keep me from fear
from hostile space
last morning I dreamt the yellow walls had melted
and I lay exposed
stretched out naked in an open field
then the eagle-people came
and trod me clawed me and swallowed me up
today I am painting the walls red
so the yellow cannot melt

I remember being pleased with the ending, thinking it was clever. Several year later I learned that I had nearly died at birth, strangled by the cord round my neck, and that I had been born at home in a room with yellow painted walls. Then the ending seemed less clever and more like a desperate attempt to achieve containment by denying what had happened and creating my own sense of safety. The beginnings of neurosis are always in defence of the self.

I say all this to make the point that in reality I have been a client all my life, in the sense that I have always found it necessary to work with my experience and to contain it and express it in some way. I think that is probably what counselling and psychotherapy are about: working with experience, expressing and mediating our response to it and finding a resolution. Certainly these are the ideas that derive from my own experience as a client and which now inform my practice as a counsellor.

Learning through Experience

My first formal contact with therapy came when I was twenty-one. I had not long been in monastic life and the isolation and monotony of the 'desert' had brought out a depression which had hounded me for years but which I had stifled behind a veneer of rosy cheerfulness. Once again I am struck by the helpfulness of my psyche in dealing with this, in that I recall I prepared a detailed account of my life and background in preparation for the initial interview. I would now recognise this as a 'history', the sort of overview of a person's life that counsellors often make at the start of working with someone. Even if I did not consciously know how to help myself, something in me knew what elements of the story to bring together.

This first therapy was short term, no more than six months all told, and was 'abreactive' or cathartic in character. The therapist concerned specialised in rebirthing and, learning through my perhaps overhelpful history, that I had suffered a birth trauma decided that the first session should be devoted to taking me through the birth experience. A co-therapist and my novice master, the priest with particular responsibility for training new monks, were present at the 'delivery'. It seemed an uncanny coincidence that the gospel reading of the day was from John: 'I tell you that you must be born over again.' (Jn: 3.8) Only as I write does it occur to me to wonder if the novice master had been guilty of a little stage management.

I will not go into the details of what was a very lengthy session, at least two hours. However, I would note that the experience involved regression and cathartic discharge of emotion. I practised yoga at the time and in the privacy of my yoga sessions I had found myself experiencing what I would now describe as pre-verbal behaviour: crawling, mouthing and groaning. Once again the unconscious process seemed to anticipate the therapeutic encounter. My recollection of the rebirthing is that it was a very powerful experience which induced elation for about six weeks (it should be remembered that I was living in an enclosed community environment at the time) only to be followed by a prolonged and even worse depression.

With experience I recognise that I escaped briefly into a kind of elated flight during which I scarcely touched earth. The experience did teach me how to be comfortable with aspects of regressed behaviour, which was invaluable later on when I became a counsellor. For example, it was easier for me to tolerate a client struggling in a regressed part of him- or herself and to allow him or her the space to do this, without feeling the need to drag him or her into a more adult part of the self. My own experience taught me that regression can be partial and focussed in the therapeutic encounter. To be unable to speak or to be contorted with rage or desperation in a counselling session does not necessarily mean the client will be unable to take charge of him- or herself at the end of the session, or to carry on with daily life until the next time. In addition, it also underlined for me the necessity of respecting the integrity of the individual's defensive system and the vital importance of the counsellor being able to interpret accurately the emotional experience of the client. I know from experience that it is not for the counsellor to induce regression and particularly not in the absence of any real knowledge of the client's inner world. My own defences were breached prematurely by this therapeutic expulsion into open space and as suggested by the words of my poem, 'the yellow did indeed begin to melt'. In other words the fragile sense of safety I had been able to construct for myself disappeared and was replaced by a black depression.

Ironically it was a real painting and decorating project which finally contributed to my leaving the monastery altogether. The silence of that endeavour helped me to reflect upon my position. It may not have escaped the reader that monastic life itself might, though not essentially, represent an attempt to return to enclosed, womb-like security. At the very least it continued my concern with the containment that stems from meaning. Containment, psychologically speaking, is that sense of emotional well-being that allows an individual to be in the world. Without containment life is frightening, confusing, even dangerous. Its roots are to be found in the earliest mother–infant relationship where mother's arms literally hold and contain the infant in a place of well-being. The distressed child who is not picked up and held runs the risk of falling into appalling desperation. Later on in life, containment can be achieved through things that give meaning to life — a sense of identity, a religious or political belief, the work that we choose to do or the relationships that we make. In counselling, containment is experienced through the reliability and consistency of the therapeutic relationship as facilitated and maintained by the counsellor. It is a key concept in my own practice.

Becoming a Counsellor

In my own case I think the wish to become a counsellor developed out of my religious concerns and my personal need to make sense of the non-sense of experience. I was still too much inside the containing archetype of God when I had my cathartic therapy to be able to consider coming out of it to take on the more down-to-earth task of dealing with flesh-and-blood people. Leaving the monastery meant losing that sense of containment but it was only several years later when I read about therapy training that I began to feel that here was something that I might be able to do.

My next formal contact with the therapeutic world came when I began training as a therapist at the Institute of Psychotherapy and Counselling, at Westminster Pastoral Foundation in London. My supervisor began the year by asking who was in therapy (it was not then a requirement). I had to say that I was not. At that time I did not recognise my own need for therapy and, as I did not have much money, stated boldly that I considered it a luxury. I was, however, firmly persuaded otherwise and began once-weekly psychotherapy with a Zurich trained Jungian therapist. This was a very different therapeutic experience. Rather than lying on the floor, I sat in an armchair. The therapist sat facing me at a distance, rather than kneeling by me and holding me as the rebirthing therapist had done. I was invited to talk rather than regress and scream. The arrangement was open ended rather than being short term.

I enjoyed the one-and-a-half years that I spent seeing this therapist. She was mid-European with the appropriate accent, and beyond her middle years. I think she rather fitted my prejudice as to what a real therapist was like. Sometimes her professor husband would let me in, discreetly, and I would be ushered into a large waiting-room crammed with wonderful objects, curios and books. It would have been quite a different emotional and therapeutic experience had I been admitted by an electric entry system, or if I had been asked to wait in a bare room.

This kind of experience has alerted me to the extent to which counselling cannot be confined to the session or to the room in which it is conducted or indeed to the person of the counsellor. For example, I used to work not far from Waterloo station, in a basement flat on a busy road. There were a number of run-down factories in the area and a general feel of inner-city decay. One day a young Canadian student was referred to me and he turned up for his assessment interview. He was very nervous and explained that he had almost turned away when he saw where I worked. He was so troubled by the general decay of the area that he felt he could have no confidence in getting the help that he needed.

In another case, a particularly difficult young woman for whom talking and communication generally was a severe problem asked if she could take an ornament from my consulting room home with her. It was a small pottery cottage and for quite a while this token would be taken away and returned at the beginning of the next session. She found it very hard both to be with me in the session and to cope with my absence between the sessions but seemed helped by the intermediary of an object which for her had taken on a special meaning.

My second therapist also brought a personal influence to bear and I know that my dreams during this period took on a markedly 'Jungian' flavour, a not uncommon phenomenon in therapies of all schools. However, I feel that my therapist actively fostered my development of a Jungian way of experiencing. For instance, she once asked me to paint a representation of the four elements, earth, air, fire and water, within a circle. I enjoyed carrying out this task and I still have the painting. I was surprised when the finished work contained not only the four elements as commissioned but also the form of a fish at their centre. This was a symbol which was appearing frequently in my dreams and seemed part of a rich emerging imagery.

I do not know where this approach would have eventually taken me for I was encouraged by my next supervisor to enter analysis, where there was likely to be more of an emphasis on working with the 'infantile transference', that part of my own earliest experience which remained unresolved and that I would project on to the person of the analyst. Thus, in my second year of training I began what turned out to be some seven years of therapy, initially twice, then three and later four times a week. It also proved to be a major influence in my transition from client to counsellor.

Naturally there were formal differences in approach to the two previous therapies. For example, I had been in analysis for six years before someone other than my therapist opened the door to me. Thus, the therapeutic experience was quite definitely concentrated between patient and therapist — that is, the analyst was careful to avoid weakening the transference by letting other people come into the picture between us. He never suggested that I should *do* anything, neither scream nor paint. I did not always like or appreciate the consistency with which he maintained the analytic framework, though the work I did with him has had more profound and lasting effects than was the case with the two previous therapists.

However, even in this formal analysis it was often the informal aspects of the relationship which mattered to me. For example, the fact that he was married and a father of children was important to me in a way which was never explicitly discussed; though there was a stage when I became very angry with the cushions that crowded his couch at a time when the endless comings and goings of wife and offspring seemed unbearably intrusive. At that point in the analysis I was feeling quite regressed and in touch with angry feelings about having to share mother. As I was regressed I was unable to say something like: 'Can't you keep your damn wife and kids away from me!' Instead I directed my angry, inarticulate feelings at the cushions on the couch which were numerous enough to represent 'something competing for space'.

On one occasion I mentioned the author Russel Hoban as I was putting on my coat to leave. My analyst had stood, which meant he would not normally say anything, but quite spontaneously he said 'I'm particularly fond of Russel Hoban.' I would come back to this event at different points during the rest of my analysis as a moment of great importance to me, though it had not been a 'therapeutic' utterance. I think this is because his simple statement had felt enthusiastic, spontaneous and authentic. At that moment the man came from behind the therapist's mask and seemed alive. Perhaps because I had felt very unstimulated by my own parents this vitality mattered a great deal to me.

I relate these details to make the point that it was not only my analyst's therapeutic behaviour that was important to me but also his impact as a person, which sometimes quite incidentally, achieved a great deal. In my own practice I find it important to remember that it is not always what use I can be as a counsellor but equally what use the client makes of me as a person that can make all the difference. It helps to keep the so-called 'expert' in me under control if I remember that it was as much the man who mattered to me in my own analysis as it was the therapist. Nor is it always a clearly positive feeling that is helpful. Recently, for example, a divorced woman in her sixties came to see me because of various family problems. She had specifically sought out a male counsellor. She negotiated a fee and contract that suited her current circumstances. In the second session she announced that she could not continue with the therapy. Something about negotiating the contract had reminded her of the severe restrictions of the early days of her marriage. I had to accept her decision but said I felt she might want to reflect on it and if at some later date she felt differently I would be happy to see her again. Within a few days I received a note asking if she could return. When she arrived for the third session she explained that having made the decision to leave she had then found herself experiencing feelings of need which she realised she could not avoid. However, by the time she attended for the fourth session she had come full circle and once again ended the work, this time for good. Subsequently she wrote saying that following the ending of the work she had gained some painful but striking insights into her self and her marriage. 'It needed a therapy situation sufficiently like my marriage and the final painful act of leaving it before I could come to my senses and begin to see what my part in the family mess has been.'

Beyond my willingness to work with this client, I feel sure that whatever therapeutic goal may have been achieved, it was not by my action as a counsellor, but rather by the use she was able to make of me as a man.

The Counsellor's Apprenticeship as a Client

So far I have described a personal interest in meaning which I feel lies at the heart of my own involvement in therapy, both as a client and as a practitioner. I have noted the natural tendency of the psyche to seek to resolve problems, which I believe to be present in all clients and to be an important part of the potential for healing. I have referred to different therapeutic experiences of my own, noting the importance of the therapist as a person in all these settings. I want to go on to consider in more detail what the apprenticeship of having been a client in these different settings has brought to my practice as a counsellor.

It is an axiom of the analytic approach to psychotherapy that the therapist cannot take the client any further in therapy than he or she has personally been taken as a client. I think it will be clear even from the brief descriptions I have given that therapies (and therapists) can have their limits, both in aim and in effect. In negotiating the transition from client to practitioner a clear sense of aims, limitations and boundaries has to be established. If we experience dependency as clients, it is all too possible to experience dominance as counsellors and, without the exercise of integrity, easy to exploit those who occupy the client role. For example, clients often identify themselves as being weak, worthless and helpless, while they think of the counsellor as being strong, important and powerful. A counsellor who is uncomfortable with his or her own feelings of weakness and helplessness may welcome the client's view of him or her as being strong and powerful and behave in such a way as to maintain that idea.

I think I probably believed that all my therapists were experts when I first went to see them. With hindsight I feel differently. The cathartic therapy, for instance, was overdetermined by the therapist — rebirthing was indicated so he simply went ahead with that. It was too bad if it cut through my defences. That was powerful. The second therapist often seemed a little too cosy in her approach, though underneath there was something which tended to suggest rather than to listen and so in a way she did dominate, even if in a more benign fashion. That too was powerful. The problem in analysis was in reverse. I think I wanted my analyst to be powerful and to speak clearly of what needed to be done but he did not. For a while I felt deprived. Here was someone I thought had the answers but who did not seem willing to share them. Eventually his unwillingness to dominate left enough space for me to find answers of my own. That was empowering.

So it is vital that the counsellor's aims are clear. 'Helping other people' as an aim is a bit vague. Helping other people to understand their own emotional and psychological responses to life, and thus alleviating their distress, is clearer. I think my different therapists differed in how much clarity of aim they had achieved. They were, I am sure, all sincere in their wish to help me, but sincerity is not enough. It has to be accompanied by respect for the client. The problem was being able to recognise respect when I got it. My analyst's dedication to maintaining his reserve and not imposing his ideas and feelings on me showed very real respect by allowing me to be central in my own analysis, but it did take me quite a while to understand this.

The rebirthing therapist genuinely wanted to help me by taking the pain of my depression away from me. In this he seemed to recognise no limits at all and showed little understanding of the depths of personal meaning which can be involved in emotional suffering. Similarly, by tending to suggest a Jungian view of things the second therapist risked imposing ideas on me which basically were not mine and which could so easily have obscured issues that mattered more directly to me.

Thus, I believe that recognising limitations is essential. For example, even if the client wants me to cure him or her, as a counsellor I must know and acknowledge that I am unable to do so. What I can do is genuinely co-operate with the client in a relationship which consistently and for a period of time seeks to uncover hidden patterns and influences which beset the client's life. By doing this, relief of symptoms, changes in behaviour and deeper self-understanding become possible.

All these benefits are achieved thanks to the integrity of the therapeutic relationship which is the genuine and responsible involvement of the counsellor with the client. The safeguard of this relationship is a clear sense of boundaries. Boundaries are the lines we all draw between ourselves and others to distinguish one thing from another, you from me, good from bad, and so on. Boundaries are essentially about respect for the other person and without them, confusion and exploitation come into play. Bringing in the novice master in the cathartic therapy, for example, was a breach of boundaries. He was an observer at this therapeutic happening and certainly not a central figure. However, simply because he was there his presence intruded upon the whole process.

In the early stage of my analysis boundaries were very strictly managed, largely I think to my benefit. However, as the years went by, there was some relaxation in this regard. I did occasionally come across members of my analyst's family, or other clients leaving as I arrived and so on. I feel enough care had been given to the establishing of boundaries that these later events could be worked with constructively.

The major problem with the analyst's consistency of practice over the years was that what he was offering did not always match what I felt I wanted or needed. In this respect analysis can be very demanding on the client.

Meeting the Client

Working in different settings with different therapeutic models, I am strongly aware in my own practice of the need for flexibility and caution in my approach to the client. My own experiences as a client underline this for me. I would say that the extent to which the therapists I have mentioned *knew* what was to be done, almost in advance of meeting me, lessened steeply from strong conviction at the cathartic end to informed not-knowing at the analytic. What I mean by this is that the rebirthing therapist seemed to have a kind of recipe which he followed to make a particular kind of cake. I felt I was really only an ingredient, albeit an important one. The analyst, on the other hand, while he clearly had his theoretical framework, kept this in the background and waited for me to tell him rather than rushing in to tell me what the problem was or what I was to do about it. I would tend to favour the latter approach in my own work as a way of ensuring that I do not dislodge the client from the central place in our work together. At the same time I am sensitive to the need to make authentic contact with clients at a level which begins to have meaning for them, because I recognise from my own client experience the importance of feeling that one is in a genuine personal relationship with the counsellor.

As clients are different, so the level of authentic contact will differ and all that is usually required is that I pay consistent and reliable attention to the client in order to achieve this. I feel that the profound depression I experienced following the rebirthing therapy, for example, stemmed in part from a failure on the part of the therapist to take the time to form any real bond with me. Thus, I experienced what happened as a powerful enactment by him which *excited* me but left me feeling empty and powerfully reminded of my own desperate helplessness. Looking back I feel the whole thing was rather poorly handled, largely because an idea, namely rebirthing, was allowed to dominate over the meeting between two people. It is as if I had been touched by a little 'godalmightyness' and then left to fall to earth, a poor crumpled creature.

By contrast my analyst would sometimes frustrate me by being rather more self-effacing than I wanted. The analyst is often referred to as a 'blank screen' on to which clients project themselves. This can suggest an almost inanimate presence, which is really a caricature of analytic reserve. In keeping him- or herself as a person out of the therapeutic arena the counsellor is really trying to leave more space for the client. It comes down to boundaries and to ensuring that what takes place in counselling has to do with clients and their needs rather than with the counsellors and their needs. It can be very tempting as a counsellor to jump into therapeutic space and drag the client along with you but it is very important to learn how to wait for the right moment. I have learned through my experience as a client and through the comments of my own clients the vital importance of being able to combine accurate analytic skill and reserve with ordinary human compassion and accessibility.

There are times when it is helpful for the counsellor to tread the middle ground between detachment and being intrusive as a person. In my own therapy this was to do with being able to believe that there really was someone there. In other words, not just a professional, or a functionary, but a flesh-and-blood individual with a life of his own. Whether this was because my own earliest models of relationship had seemed depressed, lifeless and empty, or simply because nothing ever matters to a human being if it does not feel real, it seemed important to me that a means of contact that engenders hope should ultimately emerge, in order that something reparative instead of merely adaptive (for example, 'putting a brave face on it') could develop.

The Therapeutic Relationship

This brings me to consider what it is we set out to do in counselling or psychotherapy. I am aware that part of the answer to this question will depend on the type of counselling and psychotherapy we practise: problem-solving, behavioural, analytic, and so on. That said, I feel there is still a question to answer: 'What do a client and a therapist do together?'

My own experience of different therapeutic relationships leads me to feel that a major component in the therapeutic process is the quality of the relationship which develops between the two parties and that the impact of therapy is in the here and now. If the analyst pays attention to infancy and childhood it is not to change the experience of these but to ameliorate current attitudes to them and so modify their impact. Therefore, therapy is a creative process between the client and the therapist as they make something new together out of old and familiar themes. This 'something new' is never a substitute for the experiences we have had. These stand and will always remain; if we think otherwise we are bordering on the omnipotent. The 'something new' is an adjunct to our experience which provides a way of answering it, of living with it and of living beyond it.

One of the key aspects of being in therapy is the immediacy of our involvement in the drama of the therapeutic relationship. I sometimes felt very strongly in my own analysis about the separation caused by holidays or illness, or about having to pay for help. There was not much money around in my early life and I sometimes felt anxious while in analysis that if I appeared to be doing well financially, my analyst might want to take it away from me by increasing his fee. On the other hand I felt very cared for by him through the experience of authentic 'holding' over a long period of time. All these kinds of feelings belong to what analytical psychotherapists call 'transference' and 'countertransference'. These terms refer to that special character of the therapeutic relationship by which both parties transfer feelings and conflicts which belong somewhere else on to what is going on between them. It is the task of the therapist to pay particular attention to transference–countertransference phenomena and to speak about them in a way which facilitates their being understood and resolved. If in working with a client I begin to feel drowsy or irritable, for example, I have to ask myself what might be causing this. Is it entirely my own? Perhaps I did not sleep well the night before or perhaps I have not eaten and I am feeling hungry. However, if I cannot find any explanation in myself for the feeling (and of course it could be something psychological rather than just practical), is it telling me something about the client, and what would be the most appropriate way for me to explore that?

Transference–countertransference is present irrespective of the kind of counselling being offered, it is part of what is there between people. Even if it is not to be the main focus of the work, as in the cathartic therapy I described earlier, it seems essential to me that the practitioner should know about it and be able to take appropriate account of it. As I have said, I do not think that much attention was paid to transference–countertransference in the rebirthing therapy, although as a client I remember having angry conversations with horses along country roads on the journey back from some sessions. It was never allowed for in the work that I might be angry with the therapist. This kind of experience as a client makes me all the more careful as a counsellor not to avoid difficult emotions and to allow plenty of space for them in the work itself.

As a counsellor it is my particular responsibility to be aware of my own countertransference and to make appropriate use of it. Having been on the other end of the experience as a client, it is easier for me to appreciate the experience in my own clients but it is also useful to me in coming to terms with countertransference, which can be disturbing. While a trainee, for example, I was asked by a woman client who was radically feminist why she had been given a male counsellor, as she had been assured at her assessment interview that it was more than likely she would be seen by a woman. This question, and the manner in which it was asked, immediately stirred up feelings of my own to do with negative attacking women. I felt wounded and defensive at her question and responded without thought out of my countertransference, 'I suppose you must have been lucky!' Needless to say I lost the client.

Over the years I have learned to trust the experience of countertransference as a guide in indicating where the real therapeutic issues lie or, just as importantly, where some aspect of my own material may be intruding on the process. Having experienced transference as a client, I am in a better position to recognise similarly neurotic elements which belong to me when they surface in the countertransference. In reality it has to do with knowing something of my own vulnerability from the inside and being able to tolerate it in myself and its counterpart in others. An important safeguard in this respect is, of course, the experience of supervision, a key element in therapeutic practice both during and after training. Supervision is, in many ways, the context which stands between the practitioner's experience as a client on the one hand and as a counsellor on the other. Through supervision the counsellor is enabled to explore the neurotic part of his or her own response to the client and thus, hopefully, avoids harming those he or she seeks to help.

Forever a Client

Many people looking for help do so in the hope of salvation. What they seek is healing, a cure. 'How long will it take?' they ask, implying their hope that there will be an end-point when they can stop being a client and just become 'normal' or 'well'. It might be thought that the client who becomes a counsellor is just such a person — one who has reached the finishing line and is now qualified to bring others to the same happy point.

My own view of it is rather different. Counselling is not a cure, but a context in which we can have experiences which help us to gain insight and gradually become more responsible for ourselves. That process may remove distressing symptoms of all kinds, but symptom reduction is not the end-point in itself. The achievement of counselling is not that it stops us smoking, or takes our depression away, or makes us more confident. The achievement is that it helps us to be more responsive to ourselves as whole beings, mind and body, psyche and soma. If we gain the courage to face up to our conflicts and fears rather than avoid them and push them away into symptoms, then we have made good use of counselling and we have established a bridge between what may be thought of as the client part and the counsellor part of ourselves.

It follows that the client who becomes a counsellor, as I have done, must never stop being a client, in the sense of continuing to bring the same kind of attentive listening to his or her own process. Of course, there has to be an end to formal counselling and there needs to be a balance between introspection and unselfconscious participation in life. But the client who becomes a counsellor especially has the duty of remaining in touch with his or her own inner world if he or she is to avoid abusing clients to satisfy the neurotic parts of him- or herself.

6 The Practitioner's Experience of Counselling and Psychotherapy: A Review of the Research Literature

John McLeod

The aim of this chapter is to explore and review the research literature on what it is like for counsellors and psychotherapists to practise their craft. However, the *experience* of the counsellor or psychotherapist is not a topic which has received very much systematic investigation. There is a boundless literature on what counsellors think they are doing, or what they think they should be doing (that is, theories of counselling or psychotherapy), and there has even been a fairly extensive programme of research on how counsellors actually behave in the counselling room. There has, however, been much less published on what it feels like to be doing counselling, on how the practitioner makes sense of the counselling situation, or on how these experiences change over time, as the counsellor becomes more comfortable with a particular client.

In Chapter 1, which considered the client's experience of counselling, it was suggested that there were a number of reasons for the relative absence of research into that topic. There exist serious practical, methodological and ethical difficulties associated with interviewing clients currently in counselling. Also, many psychoanalysts and behaviour therapists would take the view that experience as such could not be taken at face value or was not a legitimate subject for scientific enquiry. Although these factors certainly remain relevant in explaining the dearth of studies of the counsellor's or psychotherapist's experience, there are additional aspects of the peculiar position of the counsellor which also need to be taken into account. Thus, for example, while the client who discusses his or her experience of counselling will almost certainly be referring to one limited encounter with one counsellor, the counsellor faced with a similar task is required to filter through possibly hundreds of encounters perhaps stretching back for years. Then, many counsellors will report that when they are counselling they become immersed in the relationship with the client, and that it is extremely difficult to remember afterwards what they experienced. A therapist asked by Fitts (1965: 56–7) to write about his personal experience observed that: 'psychotherapy is a moment of complete absorption with another human being. . . . I find it difficult to describe the experience . . . after the hour, the experience is gone.' And Timms and Blampied (1985: 36) noted that 'our study of counsellors confirmed that counsellors have to struggle very hard to put their activity into words'.

The experience of the counsellor is, then, perhaps a singularly 'elusive' one (Timms and Blampied, 1985). Yet research techniques for capturing at least some of the quality of the conscious experience of the counsellor do exist (these will be discussed in the next section). So perhaps the absence of research is in part due to a resistance in counsellors to examining *in public* the experiential dimensions of their role (although a notable exception is to be found in Kottler, 1986). It is common for counsellors and psychotherapists to undertake ongoing supervision or personal therapy, in other words to engage in private and confidential exploration of the personal experience of being a counsellor. It may be that this practice to a large extent deals with the need to share and learn from each other's experiences. It is also clear that a lot of informal sharing of experience happens at training workshops and conferences (see Dryden, 1985: 1), and that counsellors and therapists tend to report that they gain a great deal from such events (see Morrow-Bradley and Elliott, 1986).

Research Strategies for Exploring the Counsellor's Experience

While writers on counselling and psychotherapy will from time to time make reference to their own personal experience with a client, there have been few research studies which have taken the practitioner's experience as a topic for systematic investigation. The studies which do exist have employed a wide variety of research techniques to unravel the 'elusiveness' of what it is like to do counselling or psychotherapy. Although this variety in approach can be seen as a tribute to the ingenuity and imagination of researchers in the field, it is at the same time indicative of a major weakness in the literature on this topic. The research on the counsellor's experience is generally fragmented and piecemeal. Few studies build on previous studies, attempt to use the same methods, or critically discuss the conclusions of previous research, and thus it is difficult to compare results and achieve an overall sense of what they mean as a whole.

The most popular technique for investigating the experience of counsellors and psychotherapists has been the rating scale. Soon after completing a session with a client, the counsellor is asked to rate, typically using a three-point or five-point scale, the extent to which certain experiences had occurred during the session. The most widely used technique in this category is Orlinsky and Howard's Therapy Session Report questionnaire, which contains 152 items covering many aspects of the therapist's perceptions of the client and of self (Orlinsky and Howard, 1977, 1986). A typical item would be: 'During this session I felt *confident* — none of the time, some of the time, a lot of the time.' The information gathered in the Therapy Session Report is subjected to the statistical technique of factor analysis, which reveals patterns and themes in the data. A recent review of the use of this method is to be found in Orlinsky and Howard (1986). A similar, but much shorter, rating-scale technique has been developed by Stiles (1980) and Stiles and Snow (1984), called the Session Evaluation Questionnaire. In this scale, therapists (or clients) are asked to rate the session on a seven-point scale between adjective pairs such as 'relaxed–tense' and 'valuable–worthless'.

The advantages of the rating-scale approach to studying practitioner experience are that it is easy to use and yields data which can be analysed using standard statistical tests. The main disadvantage of the method is that it can only offer a very rough, generalised image of what the counsellor is experiencing. As a result, other researchers have attempted to construct more sensitive, 'qualitative' techniques. Lietaer and Neirinck (1987) for example, chose to use an open-ended questionnaire, 'to let the participants formulate their experiences in their own words, in their own idiosyncratic way'. Open-ended questionnaires were also employed in the studies by Feifel and Eells (1963) and Llewelyn (1988). In a much earlier, less formal study, Fitts (1965) asked therapists to write about their experience. More recently, Elliot (1986) and Caskey et al. (1984) invited therapists to listen to tape-recorded segments of their therapy sessions and to comment on their intentions when making interventions with the client. Davis et al. (1987) carried out an innovative collaborative study of therapists' experiences of difficulty by using a peer group of therapists to generate and then discuss a large pool of examples of difficulties they had all experienced. Finally, Dryden (1985), Maluccio (1979) and Timms and Blampied (1985) carried out interviews with counsellors and psychotherapists, in which different aspects of the practitioner's experience were explored.

It can be seen, therefore, that not only are there few studies of practitioner experience available in the current literature, but that these studies have addressed different questions using different methods. In this review, the main themes and conclusions which can be derived from this body of research will be discussed, although it should be noted that caution must be exercised in making generalisations from such a limited research base.

The Dimensions of the Counsellor's Experience

One valuable aspect of large-scale factor-analytic studies such as those carried out by Orlinsky and Howard (1977, 1986) and Stiles and Snow (1984) is that they serve to define the broad parameters or dimensions of the topic being investigated, in this case what might be viewed as the core elements of the therapist's experience of doing therapy. In the research conducted by Orlinsky and Howard (1977), the experiences of seventeen 'dynamic-eclectic' therapists working with a total of thirty-two patients were investigated using the Therapy Session Report scale. Information on more than one thousand sessions was gathered from these therapists, who experienced themselves, virtually all of the time, as being *attentive* towards their clients, and saw themselves most of the time as also behaving in a *warm* and *friendly* manner. However, therapists saw themselves much less as *taking the initiative* in sessions, or *structuring* what happened in therapy. Therapists seemed to experience themselves as attempting to keep a balance between domination and control on the one hand, and acceptance or collusion on the other.

These results can be confirmed by researchers using quite different research methods. Timms and Blampied (1985: 41), for example, observed in their interviews with seventeen marriage counsellors that, although counsellors stressed the 'emergent' quality of counselling — the idea that the clients have to decide on the direction and emphasis — they were also aware of their own power to influence clients: '. . . in describing counselling the counsellors rely heavily on the first person singular of quite active verbs — steering, moving, pushing, probing, shifting, pointing out, stressing, more or less telling, selling (ideas) and so on . . . [and are attached to] the idea of cases making progress'.

In another interview study, this time with eleven social workers offering relationship counselling in the context of a family service agency, Maluccio (1979: 137) found that counsellors saw their own effective qualities as consisting of high levels of acceptance, interest, warmth and supportiveness. In this study the counsellors also exhibited a tension between control and passivity, denying that they gave advice, but listing 'giving them assignments' and 'having [the clients] read selected books' among useful activities in which they engaged with clients.

Returning to the Orlinsky and Howard (1977) research, therapists in that study reported feeling *interested, involved* and *alert* almost all of the time. One frequently reported pattern of feelings was labelled by the authors as *expansive confidence*, and consisted of the therapist feeling confident, optimistic, cheerful, relaxed, playful, effective and pleased. Slightly less often (in about half to three-quarters of sessions), therapists rated themselves as feeling *intimate* and *affectionate*. However, they also reported feeling *inadequate* and *uncertain* in one-quarter of sessions and *ill* or *disturbingly sexually attracted* in about one session in ten. Orlinsky and Howard (1977: 585) further analysed these therapist reports in terms of types of session experienced, and arrived at four different categories of session. The first they called *smooth sailing*, where the therapist sees him- or herself as warmly involved, effective and empathic, with a client who is not in distress. The second type of session they labelled *coasting*; here the therapist does not perceive him- or herself as being particularly effective, but is working with a client who is not in much apparent distress or making heavy demands. The third type of session they describe as *heavy going*, where the therapist is effective and 'expansively confident', but the client is experienced as being in severe distress. Finally, in the *foundering* category, the client is very needy but the therapist is having great difficulty in responding effectively to the client's needs. Orlinsky and Howard found that, in their sample, 17 per cent of sessions were experienced by therapists as 'heavy going' and 4 per cent as 'foundering'.

This categorisation of therapists' experiences of sessions can be usefully compared with the results of a study by Stiles and Snow (1984), in which seventeen therapists 'who represented a wide variety of theoretical orientations' used the Session Evaluation Questionnaire (a twenty-four-item rating scale which asked therapists to rate each session on dimensions such as 'difficult–easy', or 'valuable–worthless', and their own feelings on dimensions such as 'happy–sad', 'angry–pleased', and so on). These researchers found that therapists tended to evaluate sessions in terms of the *depth* achieved, and of the extent to which the session was felt to be *rough* rather than *smooth*. The therapists placed a higher value on 'deep' and 'rough' sessions. These findings are consistent with the Orlinsky–Howard data, in which therapists felt positive about 'heavy-going' sessions.

The other main area of agreement between the Orlinsky and

Howard (1977) and Stiles and Snow (1984) studies is the emphasis they place on the extent to which therapists experience their work as difficult and problematic. In these surveys, it emerged that central to the therapist's experience was how positive he or she felt about the session, how rough it was, whether he or she experienced self as 'foundering'. Thus, for example, Orlinsky and Howard report that in more than one in seven sessions their therapists experienced themselves as *frustrated*, *perplexed* or *annoyed*. It is not surprising, then, that the experience of *difficulty* in therapy has become an important and growing focus of enquiry.

The Experience of Difficulty

A very significant event within psychotherapy research was the publication in 1985 of the book *Therapists' Dilemmas* (Dryden, 1985). In that book, fourteen leading British and American therapists, representing a broad range of orientations, were interviewed about a dilemma they had experienced in the course of offering counselling and psychotherapy. Each participant was free to nominate the dilemma they wished to explore, and six different types emerged. These were:

1 *compromise* dilemmas, where a tension existed between the achievement of an ideal therapeutic aim and a more pragmatic, less risky course of action;
2 *boundary* dilemmas, around such issues as confidentiality and the appropriateness of forms of therapist behaviour;
3 *allegiance* dilemmas, concerned with adherence to particular models or schools of thought;
4 *role* dilemmas, for example the therapist as 'clinician' and 'researcher';
5 *responsibility* dilemmas, such as those occurring when working with suicidal clients; and
6 *impasse* dilemmas, referring to situations in which the therapist feels 'stuck'.

The extent to which these dilemmas can be generalised to a wider population of practitioners is a question which cannot be answered at present, and it was certainly not the aim of the initial study to provide any such general conclusions. What this study has done, however, is to initiate a new interest in the topic of the therapist's experience of difficulty.

One such piece of research, which makes reference to the seminal role of the Dryden (1985) book, is a study carried out by Davis et al.

(1987). In this investigation, a group of seven therapists, mainly eclectic in orientation, each wrote 14–20 accounts of therapeutic difficulties they had personally encountered, and then discussed these accounts collectively in order to allocate each to a manageable set of categories. The validity of this category system was then tested against a new set of accounts of reported difficulties. In the end, the group arrived at a set of nine discrete types of therapist difficulty. A particular point of interest about this research technique is that, as Davis et al. (1987: 110) observe, 'our group cohesiveness permitted us to be exceedingly open about our experiences of difficulty'.

Of the nine categories identified by Davis et al., one is similar to the Dryden (1985) 'dilemma of responsibility'. The other eight are possibly best seen as sub-categories of the 'impasse' dilemma. These eight can be briefly summarised as: feeling useless and incompetent; being concerned about damaging the client; being puzzled about how to proceed (technical perplexity); feeling threatened by the client; feeling out of rapport; experiencing the therapist's own personal issues intruding into therapy; feeling stuck and trapped; and finally, feeling thwarted or obstructed by the client. In addition, Davis et al. analysed the distribution of reported difficulties among the seven therapists contributing to the study, and found that each therapist possessed a distinctive profile of problematic experiences. One therapist, for example, experienced particular difficulty around the possibility that he might damage clients, while another found the experience of threat a major factor.

The study by Lietaer and Neirinck (1987) further explored the topic of therapist experience of difficulty by asking twenty-five person-centred therapists to note down after sessions their feelings about factors during the session which might have hindered the therapeutic process. The largest set of responses from these therapists could be categorised as failures of empathy, for example the therapist 'not being attuned to the client's experiential world', or 'focussing too little on the personal meaning of the client's message'. Another set of replies was categorised as concerned with the therapist 'reacting inadequately out of his or her own feelings', which is similar to the Davis et al. (1987) category which referred to the therapist's personal issues inappropriately influencing the session. Lietaer and Neirinck (1987) also found that some of their research participants saw themselves as hindering therapy by being either too passive or too active, which echoes the control–passivity dimension discussed earlier in relation to the work of Orlinsky and Howard (1977) and Timms and Blampied (1985).

It is clear from these studies of therapist difficulty that this kind of experience is central to the role of counsellor or psychotherapist. It would appear that perhaps for more than one-tenth of the time spent with clients, the practitioner is faced with a problem or dilemma for which there is no obvious solution. Another way of putting this is that practitioners perceive themselves as often being uncertain about how to proceed, or in danger of making mistakes, and this may be part of the reason for the reluctance until recently to place the experience of being a counsellor or therapist under public scrutiny. At this time, it is premature to suggest that the literature has yielded anything approaching a definitive or comprehensive taxonomy of difficulties. What does seem clear, however, is that the range of difficulties which have been unearthed covers a very wide spectrum indeed, from technical issues about which therapeutic tool or strategy to use, through struggles with personal feelings and self-esteem, to role and other forms of social conflict, right on to the deepest moral and ethical dilemmas.

Future Directions for Research into the Counsellor's Experience

It can be seen that some research — albeit a limited amount — has been carried out into two important aspects of the counsellor's experience: describing the varieties of feeling and behaviour which are experienced, and, more specifically, examining the types of difficulty and dilemma which counsellors and psychotherapists encounter in their work. It will be obvious to anyone with any first-hand knowledge of this field that there are many other aspects which call out for investigation and understanding. What, for example, are the distinctive facets of the experience of working with couples, or working with profoundly disturbed clients? What is the experience of success?

Before recommending studies into these and other related topics, however, it is worth considering the nature of the important questions to be asked in this field. One of the weaknesses of existing research (including research into the client's experience of counselling) has been that it has not employed any kind of consistent definition or conceptualisation of what is meant by 'experience'. Another weakness is that there has been very little attempt to understand specific elements of experience in depth — most studies seem to be trying to construct categories or identify general themes. It is possible that research into the counsellor's experience which explored the process of specific experiences, and was anchored in a systematic way of understanding experience, would result in significant progress in this area. A few brief examples will serve to illustrate these points.

To begin with the idea of exploring single aspects or elements of the practitioner's experience in more depth, it is clear that the literature contains many references to feelings and themes in counselling about which it would be valuable to know more. Thus, for example, a type of experience which has been highlighted by one writer, but not subjected to any systematic research, is that described by Symington (1983) as the therapist's 'act of inner freedom'. This type of experience happens when the therapist holds an unexamined assumption about the client which is somehow blocking progress. When the therapist is able to think about the client in a different way, when he or she has what Symington (1983) calls a 'moment of illumination', then the therapeutic process is able to move and progress. An example Symington offers is of a client who was paying little more than half of what his other patients were charged. He writes, 'I had resigned myself to it in the same way as I reluctantly resign myself to the English weather.' But then, 'one day a startling thought occurred to me: "Why can't Miss M pay the same as all my other patients?"' His 'inner attitude' towards her had changed, and this subsequently triggered changes in her attitude to herself as she worked on accepting herself as someone who *could* pay the full price. Now, it would be very interesting to know if Symington's 'act of inner freedom' is something which many counsellors and therapists experience, and, if it is, what are the processes by which it occurs.

Another area of counsellor experience which is infrequently referred to in the literature, but which is potentially of great significance, is the counsellor's sense of being a member of an organisation, and what it means for a counsellor or psychotherapist to have a role within an agency. Almost all writing on counselling makes an implicit assumption that counselling is a matter of what happens between the practitioner and the client. Crandall and Allen (1982), by contrast, have begun to describe some of the organisational processes which might influence the behaviour or experience of a counsellor, for example the organisation having rules or goals which are difficult to reconcile with the needs of a particular client, or the mirroring in counsellor–client relationships of the types of relationship offered at a supervisor–counsellor level. There is clearly great scope for studying the experience of being a counsellor or psychotherapist in different types of agency or organisation, and such research has practical implications in terms of the management of counselling services.

Moving on to the theoretical or conceptual basis of research into the counsellor's (or client's) experience, there are at least two theoretical models which could be employed to illuminate work in this area. The first is Kolb's Experiential Learning model, which depicts a holistic cycle of learning through experience in which the learner may initially be aware of a learning task at a concrete, feeling or physical level, then reflects upon his or her concrete experience, then attempts to relate this reflection to more abstract principles or theories, and then acts upon this new framework for understanding, thus producing a new set of concrete experiences (see Kolb and Fry, 1975). An interesting facet of the Kolb model is that it predicts that individual learners tend to have been socialised into 'specialising' in one or perhaps two phases of the cycle. Thus, for example, someone might be good at 'abstract conceptualisation' but uncomfortable with 'active experimentation'. In many ways Kolb's model of experiential learning, or the experience of problem-solving, is too simple, but it does begin to suggest ways in which the experiential *process* of practising counselling might be understood: for instance, do effective practitioners experience themselves as moving through these stages in their work with clients?

A second useful theoretical perspective is that provided by existential-phenomenological psychology (see Valle and King, 1978). This tradition in philosophy and psychology dates back to the nineteenth century, and takes as its main objective the description and understanding of human experience. Existential psychologists suggest that it makes sense to view experience as consisting of three interlocking aspects: the individual's experience of being with self, the individual's experience of being with others, and the individual's experience of being with the physical world, in particular his or her body. A powerful example of the way in which this perspective can be applied is to be found in the early work of Laing (1960, 1961). Laing was, of course, attempting to make sense of the experience of people labelled as 'schizophrenic', but his combination of phenomenological methods of enquiry and careful analysis of these three aspects of experience could be equally effective in opening up the inner world of counselling.

Differences between the Counsellor's and the Client's Experience of Counselling

In this final section, a slightly different topic will be discussed. Until now, the focus has been on the counsellor's experience, defined in terms of his or her individual reporting of thoughts and feelings. But the experience of practising counselling is very much one of being *in relationship*. The fact that counsellor and client are in a relationship is so obvious that most practitioners would take it for granted. What is less straightforward, however, is the notion that the relationship is different for each party. Again, to some extent this is obvious — one is helping and the other is being helped; one is paid and the other is paying; one is (supposedly) congruent and the other may be incongruent. In this section it will be suggested that there are a number of important differences between the client's and the counsellor's experience of the same relationship and that a fuller understanding of this process is required.

Few studies of the counsellor's experience have attempted to assess the level of agreement between the different perspectives taken by practitioner and client. In a pioneering early study of this topic, Blaine and McArthur (1958) asked two psychiatrist–patient pairs to give their separate accounts of what happened during therapy. The researchers concluded that these patients and their therapists possessed quite different perspectives on the meaning of the same events. One therapist, for example, believed that what was discussed during some of the sessions was particularly significant because of his interpretations of 'the existence in the unconscious of passive "needs", incestuous wishes and large amounts of irrational hostility'. His client, on the other hand, thought that what was helpful in these sessions was the 'therapist stating that there must be a reason for his symptoms' (Blaine and McArthur, 1958: 346).

In another early study, Feifel and Eells (1963) asked twenty-eight psychoanalytically oriented therapists and their clients to complete an open-ended questionnaire enquiring about aspects of their experiences in therapy. When asked about the aspects of therapy which had been particularly *helpful*, the clients tended to reply that they believed they had been helped primarily by the opportunity to talk over problems, while the therapists saw the most helpful factor as being their mastery of skill and technique. A similar result was found by Kaschak (1978) in a study of fifteen mainly eclectic psychotherapists and their clients. In a recent study of this type, Llewelyn (1988) examined the relationship between twenty-two therapists (again, predominantly eclectic in orientation) in terms of what they each felt to have been the most helpful events in therapy. In this study the clients reported being helped most by reassurance and problem-solving, while the therapists emphasised the helpfulness of insight.

Some studies have identified a number of other specific differences in client and counsellor experiences and perspectives. Hunt (1985) and Maluccio (1979) suggest that in the first meeting the counsellor may be concerned with general issues of assessment, while the client is concerned with his or her current level of distress. Brannen and Collard (1982), Hunt (1985), Maluccio (1979) and Mayer and Timms (1970) all comment on the different assumptions sometimes made by clients and counsellors regarding what kind of help is on offer — clients often seek advice, while counsellors usually see 'talking' as the most effective way to solve problems. This observation is reinforced by the results of a study by Murphy et al. (1984), in which psychotherapy clients were asked to identify the factors they felt had helped them most in their treatment. The most frequently cited factor was 'advice' from the therapist. Caskey et al. (1984) carried out a study in which both clients and therapists listened to taped excerpts from sessions and then gave their estimates of what the therapist's *intentions* were each time he or she said something, and how *helpful* these interventions were. Results suggested, on the whole, that 'therapists had little awareness of the immediate impact of their responses' (Caskey et al., 1984: 288). Finally, Maluccio (1979) found significant differences in clients' and therapists' evaluations of the overall effectiveness of therapy, with clients generally being more satisfied than their therapists with the eventual outcome.

All these studies demonstrate important differences between the experience of being a client and that of being a therapist. It would appear that each role is associated with a distinct perspective on the events which occur in the context of the relationship. Blaine and McArthur (1958), for example, emphasise the immersion of the therapist in the technique of therapy, while for the client it is a much more personal and down-to-earth process: 'the chance to discuss themselves with an impartial, intelligent, "safe" person'. Maluccio (1979) emphasises the fact that clients tend to see events and relationships in their life outside the therapy room as being important in triggering change, while therapists are less aware of these 'outside' factors, and place more importance on what happens in therapy itself.

However, although some significant differences in perspective have been identified, the research to date has not been able to penetrate deeply enough into the process of interaction between client and counsellor or therapist to discover what these differences mean in practice, and how the therapist or client deals with them. Clearly, if successful therapy involves client and therapist working together, to form a therapeutic *alliance*, then it is essential that differences in perspective are minimised or worked through. On the other hand, Llewelyn (1988: 235) suggests that discrepancy in perspective may actually be useful, since it 'confronts the client with the need to behave in a different way'.

Finally, it could be argued that none of the research on practitioner–client differences in perspective has adequately reflected the complexity of the problem. Within a relationship, for example, each person not only experiences and perceives the other, but also has a view about how he or she is perceived or experienced by the other. Quite possibly, he or she also has a sense of what the other thinks and feels about how he or she feels about them. Laing and his colleagues (Laing et al., 1966) called this kind of process a 'spiral of metaperspectives'. In their own work this idea was applied to families and couples, but it could be just as easily applied to the counsellor–client relationship. In this case, an exploration of the counsellor's experience of being in a relationship with a client might produce something like the following:

> *Counsellor*: I am trying to listen to what the client is really saying.
> *Client*: I am aware that the counsellor is listening to me.
> *Counsellor*: I don't know if the client appreciates the fact that, although I haven't said much, I am actively listening.
> *Client*: He doesn't seem to realise that I understand what he is trying to do.

This is a very brief example of the kind of metaperspectives which might be in operation during one rather undramatic moment in counselling. It should be clear that, when metaperspectives are taken into account, there are many opportunities in counselling for mutual misunderstanding to occur between client and practitioner. In the example above, for instance, the counsellor and client are in agreement in terms of their direct perceptions of each other, but disagree at the 'meta' level of wondering what the other thinks. It is possible that an application of the Laing et al. (1966) model to the problem of counsellor–client differences in perspective might help to clarify many of the instances of counsellor difficulty or stuckness discussed earlier. It is also an approach which demonstrates the importance of taking experience not in isolation but always as experience *in relation* to another person or object.

Conclusions

This review of the research literature on the practitioner's experience of counselling or psychotherapy is largely the story of an absence. Very little research has been done, and there are few signs that much more is likely to be completed in the future. Recent publications reflecting the 'state of the art' in psychotherapy research (for example, Greenberg and Pinsof, 1986; Rice and Greenberg, 1984) demonstrate that a great deal of energy and attention is being lavished on research into client processes, significant events in therapy and therapist interventions defined in terms of response style. There has been an extensive literature on client and therapist *experiencing* which has investigated the relationship between the depth of experiential processing exhibited by each person and the effectiveness of the session (Klein et al. 1986), but in this work 'experiencing' is taken to be a variable which can be rated by external judges or observers listening to tape-recorded therapy segments: there is no attempt to ask either therapist or client what the experience is like for them!

Yet it is to be hoped that this review has been able to establish the potential value of research into the practitioner's experience. There are three direct ways in which further research in this area can be of benefit. First, studies of what it is like to be doing counselling or therapy are almost certainly going to be of more interest to practitioners than are studies which take the perspective of a detached observer. Thus, compared with much research which is currently published in journals, research into counsellor experience may well be more accessible, applicable and relevant to practitioners, thus overcoming the resistance of practising therapists to reading and using research findings (Morrow-Bradley and Elliott, 1986). Secondly, research into counsellor experience is useful for supervisors and trainers, in sensitising them, for example, to the kinds of difficulties which are most often encountered, in facilitating trainee disclosure of difficulties and in designing training programmes. Probably most important of all, however, is the contribution that research on counsellor experience can make, when taken together with research on client experience, in helping to develop awareness of the ways in which the client's world and the counsellor's world can so easily diverge, leading to counselling in which the real concerns of the client are muffled and hidden.

7 The Counsellor's Experience of Failure

Dave Mearns

A Failure

> *Ann [the client, speaking to her counsellor]*: You don't *really* care! This is
> just a bloody game for you. You're so damned at ease. I'm breaking
> up here, and you're so damned at ease. . . . You're not really 'with'
> me at all. I don't need this. . . . [*Ann leaves*]

It is easy to regard this as a 'dramatic exit' by a client who is
struggling with commitment, or an example of the client's 'transference' of childhood experiences on to the counsellor resulting in the
client rejecting the 'parent-like' figure who is not perfect. Auto-
matic assumptions such as these protect the counsellor from feelings
of failure but further dismiss, and may even *abuse*, the client.

As it happens, in the above example, Ann was quite correct in her
perception of the counsellor. The counsellor had aimed to form a
relationship with Ann in which he was fully involved with her in
everything she chose to explore. He had failed to do that and the
process had failed. Ann did not come to her next appointment.

In any relationship both people contribute to the pattern which
evolves but the counselling relationship is special in that it is
unequal. Consequently, we require the counsellor to pay particular
attention to her own contribution to the relationship, and, having
done that, she may invite the client to explore what he can learn
about himself through considering *his* part in the relationship with
the counsellor. In both psychodynamic and person-centred counselling particular use is made of the relationship between counsellor
and client. However, in his work with Ann the counsellor, who is
also the writer, had failed so abysmally to establish a vibrant
relationship that the client did not have the opportunity to make
such discoveries. This failure could even have been predicted, for in
the case notes from the previous meeting we find evidence of the
counsellor's concern about his work.

> . . . What am I really doing? She is placing so much faith in me — and
> what I have to offer seems so shallow. Am I getting so comfortable with
> clients' torment that I don't feel it any more? I feel that she wants more

from me and I am not able to be as fully involved as she wants . . . and she is the third client with whom I've felt that in recent times.

Following Ann's dramatic exit, the counsellor writes:

Ann is right — my senses *have* dulled. As I have got more experienced and 'clever', I've become duller and less immediate in my experiencing and relating with clients. When the quality of my 'presence' and 'spontaneity' was most of what I had to offer clients, I needed it and used it well — but now that I have developed a professional repertoire of skills those qualities are less sustained. And Ann isn't the only one who has suffered — there are some others who haven't moved on as quickly or as surely as they might. . . . I am in danger of becoming the very thing I fear most — the *detached* counsellor.

What *Is* Failure?

If counselling was simply a matter of applying a set of techniques in a prescribed order and a defined manner, then assessing *failure* would merely imply comparing the counsellor's behaviour with a prescribed schedule. However, people and their problems are not so easily programmed. Ann resented the counsellor's calm, easy manner, feeling that it lacked the immediacy and intensity which would be helpful for her. And yet, with another client, that same counsellor passivity in the face of torment might be a quality which was valued by the client. Ann's reaction illustrates the human variability of counselling which resists any attempts to reduce it to a 'programme'. In his work with Ann, the counsellor followed what would generally be regarded as an appropriate programme, and the result was failure.

As part of the research for this chapter the writer sent short questionnaires to seventy-five counsellors and therapists world-wide. The results of this investigation will be explored in more detail later, but for now it is relevant to note that all but one of the sixty-one returns acknowledged the existence of failure. However, they did not find it easy to distinguish the counsellor's responsibility for failure. One of the counsellors described two categories of failure, the first of which we might call *circumstantial failure*:

. . . any counsellor, no matter of what persuasion or how skilful, is inevitably going to fail with some clients because of factors beyond both the counsellor's and client's control such as personalities, timing, environmental factors, the intractable nature of so many difficulties and, above all, our limited understanding of the complexities of the human psyche.

He distinguishes this from what we might call *counsellor failure*, which he describes as 'a recognised mistake of the counsellor arising from such factors as insensitivity, fatigue, bad timing, low level of empathy, abuse of power and meeting the counsellor's needs rather than those of the client'. The apparent neatness of this distinction might help counsellors in their consideration of the locus of responsibility, but it masks the fact that failure is an *experience* of counsellor and client and as such it involves feelings as much as thoughts. So, even though the counsellor may think about the event and decide that *circumstantial failure* is an appropriate label, the likelihood is that his feelings will still be asking him the question: 'But could I not have done something more?'

A strictly logical way of defining failure is in terms of *expectations not met*. The client and counsellor embark upon the process with certain expectations as to what that 'process' will be, and perhaps also about its products — what it should achieve. Whether client and counsellor agree on the appropriateness of the term *failure* or not depends largely upon the similarity of their expectations. It is not at all uncommon for a counsellor to feel very pleased about her work with a client and to be surprised when the client terminates because he was not getting what he wanted. Equally, there are instances when the counsellor is astonished to hear the client's positive evaluation of a counselling process which the counsellor had largely viewed as being unproductive. There is an excellent example of this presented in another book in this series (Mearns and Thorne, 1988: 31) where, in response to the counsellor's expression of uncertainty and curiosity about the benefit the client had been drawing from the seven sessions thus far, the client said:

> . . . what have I been getting out of it? Wow! . . . It has just kept me alive, that's all! I often go round and round in circles when I'm with you, and it seems like I'm getting nowhere, but all the time I'm being *me*. I'm being what I can't risk with anyone else — I'm being confused, distraught . . . crazy. I mean, I know now that I'm not crazy . . . but I didn't know that before. It feels like the more I can just be these things with you, then the less frightened I am of them . . . the less frightened I am of me.

In this extract it appears that the client had been considering the question of success or failure in terms of the *process* of the relationship between himself and the counsellor, while the counsellor had been concerned with the immediate *products* of their work. When the counsellor could not see obvious changes in the client's behaviour or attitudes, she was ready to assume failure.

This *process* versus *product* dichotomy should play an important part in the early discussions between counsellor and client when they are examining the expectations which each has for their work together. Such discussion might come in the first session, or perhaps the second meeting is a more appropriate time to compare perspectives since by then the client has been able to get a measure of support and also both parties have had some time to understand each other. Even then, the details of such expectations cannot be compared fully at that early juncture. Were the counsellor to try to explain some of the more intricate and important aspects of the therapeutic *process*, then it would not be surprising if she received a polite nod of mystification from her client. This does not remove from the counsellor the onus of *trying* to explain, but simply emphasises that the issue of expectations and differences in expectations is a therapeutic item which requires repeated re-visitation: indeed, such re-visiting often generates further important therapeutic material, for example:

> *Client*: I realise that it has been important that we had another look at what we both expected. What I am seeing now is that all along, at some level, I've been expecting to become dramatically *happy* in my life . . . like the ending would be as it is in fairy-tales. I see now that that expectation may belong more to fiction than real life.

The most common configuration of expectations is for the counsellor to be more concerned with process and the client with product. The client may be saying 'Help me to get rid of my eczema'/'Help me to get my marriage together again'/'Make me confident'. In relation to any of these the counsellor may be saying 'I would like to be supportive and gently insightful in such a way that is most likely to help you to explore all the elements of your present and past life which come to bear on your present difficulties.' The counsellor's expectation reflects the fact that she cannot take responsibility for the client achieving the products he desires since that depends in large measure on the client's actions and motivation. The client, on the other hand, may be coming to counselling with the view that it is like conventional medicine to which one surrenders oneself totally but in return expects to be cured. The issues which are most prone to create a sense of failure are those where the expected product is very clear and demanding like an addiction to alcohol or drugs, or physical symptoms of anxiety or depression. It is not surprising that the client, and perhaps other parties, place great store on the eradication of that behaviour. While behavioural counselling responds to that demand by endeavouring to meet it head on, most other approaches are concerned to treat the whole person and not just the behaviour. Unless clarification of expectations is achieved the possibilities of 'failure' are high. Books on psychodynamic counselling are riddled with examples where clients left with the feeling that 'nothing had changed', and huge feelings of resentment towards the counsellor, who for her part is frustrated by the fact that the client has left before they have been able to complete the process. Similarly, in the person-centred domain, the writer was amused by one client whose response to the counsellor's detailed description of the importance of the 'therapeutic relationship' was to say '*relationship* . . . the last thing I need is another one of them!'

Our emphasis so far has naturally been on the counsellor and what he or she can do, but the client has more power over the success or failure of counselling. The writer remembers work with one client where the process seemed to move perfectly even to that point where the counsellor has that, often unvoiced, feeling that success is virtually inevitable. At precisely that point the client terminated, but fortunately not without explanation. . . .

> I realised after our last meeting that I had to stop. I know it is not the right thing for me to do . . . and yet it is what I am going to do. I am finding myself galloping along a road . . . and I can see clearly ahead that that road leads to the end of my marriage and the possibility is that I may lose my children as well. The road also leads to a much healthier *me* than I ever felt possible, but it is not a road that I can take just now.

Apart from helping the client to look at all aspects of this, there is no other way to respond to it except with respect.

In what Circumstances do Counsellors Experience Failure?

Reference was made in the previous section to the questionnaire which was sent to seventy-five counsellors and therapists world-wide. This questionnaire consisted of only three questions, but these were quite searching and when answered fully they involved a fair degree of self-disclosure. The questions were:

1 In what kind of circumstances do you experience failure as a counsellor/therapist?
2 What is that 'experience' of failure actually like for you? Describe it in whatever ways are meaningful to you.
3 How do you usually respond to this experience of failure? What do you do?

The covering letter informed the counsellors and therapists about the purpose of the investigation and promised anonymity. Included in the package for British participants was a return envelope with first-class postage.

Since this was an open-ended exploration rather than an attempt to test hypotheses, it was more important to choose a sample of counsellors and therapists who might respond as fully and openly as possible to these revealing questions rather than endeavouring to achieve a 'representative' sample of workers. Hence, the single criterion used in the selection of the sample was that they should be counsellors and therapists who knew the writer well enough for him to sign the letter with his Christian name. As might be expected with this personal form of sampling the level of return was quite high — sixty-one (81 per cent) ranging as far abroad as Australia and consisting chiefly of person-centred and psychodynamic practitioners of varied experience. Although the questionnaire was anonymous, almost all the respondents added their names. In a few cases these responses were followed up by letter or telephone in the search for more detail.

The Disappearing Client

By far the most common circumstance in which these counsellors and therapists experienced failure was where the client 'disappeared without communication'. Counsellors noted that such disappearance was most often after the first meeting and although it was quite easy to rationalise this in terms of the client simply finding that counselling was not what they expected, there still seemed to be a fair degree of discomfort and self-questioning aroused in many counsellors. However, an even more potent circumstance was where the client disappeared without any explanation after several sessions of work. The feeling of failure was intensified when the counsellor had invested particular effort in the relationship.

Problems of Involvement

A sense of failure can arise when the counsellor feels unable to establish sufficient *trust* with the client to be allowed to see him as he sees himself without defences. As one counsellor said: 'I feel bad if clients are going to bad places and won't let me come.' Another counsellor refers to this as a failure to establish a 'personal working alliance'.

While counsellors can feel frustration and failure where clients are reluctant to become fully involved with them, similar feelings of frustration and failure can result from the exact opposite circumstance — where the client wants *more* from the counsellor than she feels she can give. For example, a student counsellor writes:

> In our first session, John [the client] was very quiet and withdrawn — so much so that I was pretty sure he wouldn't come back. But he did, and about half-way through our second session he broke down completely. It was as though he had been trying to hold back his feelings and eventually had just let go. At first I felt pleased that we had broken through, but then rapidly I began to feel a kind of terror. I realised that he is the very client with whom our counselling service can't cope. It can deal with the client who gives a little, but when a client really gives everything it can't service that enormous need. To see a client once a week for ten weeks

would normally be regarded as a maximum, but John needed much more than that. At the very minimum he needed someone to be available to him for some time during each day, and perhaps more than that. The real frustration and sense of failure comes from feeling that I would want to, and could, work at that intense level with him, but effectively I am prevented from doing so. The 'terror' in that kind of failure is realising that having helped him to open up I shall soon be sitting with him exploring psychiatric ways of closing him down.

Not Being Good Enough

An obvious circumstance in which counsellors may feel failure is where they have identified themselves as 'not being good enough', 'making a mistake' or 'missing opportunities'. The questionnaires yielded numerous examples of this, most of which centred around the counsellor identifying ways in which her own needs or fears had become over-involved in the relationship with her client, for example: 'I feel a failure when I find myself reacting over-emotionally to a client's manipulation so that I can't get past my own feelings of anger, frustration or hurt to respond to him or her.' Another counsellor referred to a similar experience of getting 'caught' by the client's games:

> I feel failure when I don't have the energy or vigilance to stay in touch with myself but instead get 'caught' by the client and respond to them as people normally do — this can be protectively, or doing too much, or punitively . . . the possibilities are endless, depending on the client.

Still in this category of personal inadequacies which counsellors identified, there was frequent mention not simply of getting stuck in the client's pattern of relating, but sometimes even *causing* that stuckness in the client through the counsellor's personal needs or projections becoming involved, for example:

> I had worked with George for four years — longer than I have worked with any other client. George had also been important to me because he was the first client with whom I had been through a deep counselling experience. But in the end I nearly failed George. It was so important to my professional self-esteem that George was a 'success', that I would over-react every time he got depressed or found things difficult. I was glad that I was in the habit of making tapes of my work because it was only on listening to these that I was able to hear myself 'jollying' him along and essentially denying all of the difficulties he was expressing. I *needed* him to be healthy, and was scared to see anything else — it got to the stage where I really wasn't 'working' with him at all.

Fear

As well as these forms of 'stuckness' which arise either from the counsellor getting embroiled in the client's pathology or introducing her own, there is one source of failure which is so striking that it deserves special mention. One of the most paralysing experiences for a counsellor is the feeling of *fear*. In mild doses some fear is to be expected as a counsellor embarks on quite personal and demanding work with a relative stranger. Moderate amounts of fear can also arise where the counsellor feels pressured by a demanding and perhaps socially powerful client. Fear inhibits the counsellor and can induce what the writer calls 'counsellor paralysis' where the counsellor finds it difficult to listen, understand and respond in an authentic manner, but instead becomes over-deliberate and guarded in her actions. These forms of fear are quite common and regularly receive attention in training and supervision. However, there is a much greater fear which appears to be almost totally debilitating, and that is where the counsellor actually fears the intensity and depth of the client's feelings of anger or violence. In some such instances the counsellors in our sample defined their work as 'failing', but did not seem too regretful of that fact, for example:

> Now and again with a client I have felt real fear. One such client was very quiet and polite, but his eyes registered nothing but coldness, anger and violence. I was shit-scared of him from the very beginning. We had three sessions together, which was one more than I wanted. In that time I parcelled up his problem very neatly, gave him lots of advice and smiled at him every ten seconds.

The 'Dumping Client'

Fear can also be present in the special case of the client who uses counselling as a brief stopping point for the 'dumping' of powerful feelings. The dumping client rarely comes for more than one session at a time and never for more than two. Usually the content of these sessions is heavily laden with paranoia, aggression and even violence. In one such session a client of the writer described in increasingly lurid detail how he was about to kill and dismember his wife and children. One of the problems with dumping clients is that it is difficult to be sure of the dynamic which is operating for them, because they do not come back. It is as though they have used the single session to off-load the most powerful parts of their emotional existence without any particular intention to do more than that. The poor counsellor can be left carrying much of that enormous burden — for instance, in the above case the writer found himself utilising whole sessions with two separate supervisors before some measure of stability could be re-established. Dumping clients are difficult to avoid because they cannot be spotted in advance, but private practitioners are advised to charge them double if at all possible!

Impotence

Another circumstance in which the counsellor experiences a sense of failure is not so much related to personal or professional inadequacy, but to her relative *impotence* compared to the degree of disturbance of her client or to the other life pressures which dominate the client and inhibit growth. For instance, in working with the chronically mentally ill the worker might have to adjust her criteria of success or failure or else she might find herself failing with everybody. Rather than seek a dramatic impact on every patient, smaller gains in the direction of improving coping become the emphasis. The situation can be just as frustrating in counselling work with clients who are trapped by poverty or family pressures. Also, while anti-depressants can help some clients to engage in counselling, other medications, particularly the major and minor tranquillisers, can be a source of frustration and seeming failure, as one counsellor reported:

> Nowadays I've virtually made it a rule that I don't see anybody while they are on reasonably heavy doses of tranquillisers. I know that a general rule such as this will be closing the door to some people who might be helped, but I really feel that, in general, counselling with those on heavy medication is a recipe for failure. There is nothing more frustrating than having ten very productive sessions with a client, and seeing him make tremendous movement, then finding that he does not really believe that *he* made that progress, but it was 'him on drugs' that did it.

Suicide

There is one final important circumstance in which the counsellor can experience failure, and that is where her client commits suicide. It is *extremely rare* for clients to commit suicide while in counselling or therapy. In a sense the two behaviours of being in counselling and committing suicide are opposites with the one carrying 'hope' and the other not. A more common paradigm is for the client to terminate counselling and commit suicide some months thereafter. Although the counsellor has no designated responsibility for, or to, this former client, there will still be feelings, and often feelings of failure. We end this section with an account of one such incident and begin the next part of the chapter with a record of the counsellor's thoughts and feelings.

> Some hurts just don't go away. I've been round this hundreds of times, and every time I come to the same answer — that it could not have worked out any other way.
>   Robert came to see me three times. I remember him so clearly — especially his coldness. I remember once feeling 'this man is already dead'. He was like a lifeless body — so stiff and dead — he would walk

in, sit down and *try* to talk. On his second visit I thought he was about to cry for himself. I really wished he would, but he wiped his eyes and returned to his seemingly dispassionate way of being. It was the first time that that word 'dispassionate' had ever carried any meaning for me. I actually *tried* to get him to cry. But I think my 'tricks' actually put him off — I've worried about that.

At the end of the third meeting I knew Robert was not going to come back. If only I had had the courage actually to voice that — to try to work with that. It was an unspoken feeling, but I am sure we both felt it and knew that the other felt it. God, why didn't I have the courage!

Two days before our fourth appointment I received a letter from Robert thanking me very sincerely for my help, but saying that he did not think that counselling was the right thing for him at this time in his life. Three months after that letter I read in the local newspaper about this man called 'Robert' who had sat on the main train line and blown his head off with a shotgun. The article said that this method of suicide was 'the act of a very determined man'.

What is the *Experience* of Failure?

Robert's counsellor describes her experience of failure:

I remember clearly my first thoughts and feelings, and as time has passed I have returned to these as probably the most accurate. I was desperately sad at the thought of Robert so deliberately making sure that he killed himself. And I was so so frustrated that he had not let me 'in'. But also I knew that he was probably 'too far gone' to let anybody in. That was what he had been exploring with me — and he concluded that 'counselling is not the right thing for me at this time in my life'.

After this initial clarity I spent the next few years going round all the other alternatives. I suppose I went through my own *transition* process with respect to his death. At first I did not tell anyone — that was a kind of 'denial' underlayed with a thick coating of guilt. I wish I had been able to get it out right away, because it festered for a while, and I know my work was pretty uninspiring at that time. I suppose I couldn't risk being really 'present' with clients, so I was virtually 'absent'. I really should not have been working at all. Eventually I started to cry — then it all came out — by myself at first — and then, almost compulsively, I had to tell other people. I actually chose to go to a couple of 'encounter-group' weekends because I knew that I would be able to talk about it there. After that, there were lots of feelings about my inadequacies, but mostly about the fact that I had not been able to be there, just as another human being, for Robert. I had tried to get him to let go his feelings, but I did not give him a real person with whom to do it.

Time *has* healed the hurts, and I realise that Robert was pretty far gone before he met me, but I do feel that his death has created one little thing — it has helped me to find a personal depth which I never had before.

A recent book by Rosemary Dinnage (1988) is instructive on *clients'* experiences of failure. Many of the people she interviewed had felt disempowered, sometimes even abused, and often entrapped by their therapists. In our present investigation, which involved mainly person-centred and psychodynamic counsellors, the experiences of failure were quite different and much more varied. Almost all the counsellors wrote about both thoughts and feelings, with the two often contradicting each other.

Thoughts

Characteristically, the thoughts were concerned with considering not just what the counsellor might have done wrong but all the other possible reasons for apparent failure. The counsellors in the survey were knowledgeable enough to realise that their considered conclusions might equally well be classified as 'rationalisations'. For instance, 'I don't fail — the client does'/'obviously the client was not ready for counselling at this time'/'I think she was probably looking for a counsellor of a different sex from me'/'I'm really glad I laid it on the line for him — at least now he knows that if he's coming into counselling it's got to be serious'/and, 'Well it's better that she finds out now rather than after spending a lot of money!'

Another 'thinking' strategy is to focus on other successes. This has always been a favourite of the writer, who consequently urges trainees to make sure that they are working with at least three or four clients at any one time, so that if they are experiencing failure in one or two then there are others to think of to maintain some element of courage and self-esteem. Furthermore, there is nothing worse for a trainee counsellor than to be working with only one client where so much of the trainee's developing professional self-respect becomes invested in that one relationship that they become paralysed and almost certainly fail.

Feelings

While the various thinking strategies help to keep counsellors afloat during experiences of failure, they are counterbalanced by the affective domain. In our sample there was an enormous variety of responses to the 'disappearing client' which was the 'failure' experience described by most of the counsellors. In reading these varied accounts the writer could not help thinking that they were each in their own way representing recurrent feelings from childhood. Some even made that connection themselves: 'I feel "little"' — 'some connection with "childlike"' and 'In most other ways I function quite professionally, but when I feel that rejection it takes me right back into childhood.'

One counsellor gives us a simple and almost poetic account of the variety of her feelings in failure: 'Feeling bleak and grey —

sometimes stupid, sometimes dishonest. Weary. A bit depressed. Annoyed with myself. Fed-up.' A number of counsellors mentioned the tripartite of 'sad/guilty/angry'. These three feelings often seemed to occur in that order and looked as though they were representing, in the language of Transactional Analysis, the responses from the three ego-states of Adult, Child and Parent: 'I am sad that we are not going to be able to continue our work together'/'I feel guilty that I may have done something wrong'/and 'I am angry at the client for not trying hard enough.'

Counsellors also spoke of feelings that might be commonly associated with 'unfinished business'; indeed, one counsellor reported a classical Zeigarnik Effect[1] in describing how she sometimes fantasised on what would happen if the client returned and also fantasised on the process of saying goodbye which of course had been denied to her. Feelings of 'frustration' and 'impotence' were frequently mentioned as well as two beautiful quotations from the same, very literary therapist: 'It is like an unfinished Gestalt that niggles distressingly at my consciousness' and 'I feel like Bowlby's babies did — protest, despair and finally detachment.' The incompleteness of the process can also leave the counsellor feeling a burden from the unfinished business — a sense of 'contamination' probably relating to what the counsellor was still carrying for the client.

The experience of failure can make counsellors feel very bad indeed. Counselling is such a private and personal activity that failure can hurt very deeply and make the helper doubt the very essence of her ability. Perhaps the experience is intensified because counsellors tend to be intropunitive (see Lietaer and Neirinck, 1987). Two of the respondents to the questionnaire were among the most prominent counsellors in Britain, and yet in this section on their experience of failure they wrote: 'It sometimes makes me doubt my ability as a counsellor, and that feels bad'; and 'If I am particularly tired or drained a failure can push me to irrational thoughts of packing it all in and returning to business or burying myself in administration.'

What do Counsellors *do* in Response to the Experience of Failure?

The fact that failure can cut so deeply is further justification for the importance which counselling in Britain attaches to *supervision*. Most respondents to our questionnaire emphasised the use they made of their supervisor in the event of failure. Indeed, an important criterion in selecting a supervisor is that the chosen person should be one with whom the counsellor feels sufficiently at ease to explore even the most tortuous elements of self-doubt. For this reason, line-managers make poor supervisors!

As well as using the supervisor, counsellors go through quite a bit of thinking work in response to the experience of failure. Some of this, as was mentioned in the previous section, is difficult to separate from rationalisation, but there is also serious consideration given to questions like: 'Why has the client gone?' and 'What could I have done differently?' Counsellors may also engage in some *research*. Thus, for example, when a counsellor is faced with a client carrying a diagnostic label like 'psychotic', 'anorexic', 'addict' or 'sexually abused', there can be a fear in the counsellor's mind that there may be very special facets of this phenomenon that perhaps she does not know. Researching these as a response to an experience of suspected failure is perfectly responsible although not necessarily fruitful. While such investigation may help her to understand the range of possibilities in clients with such labels it does not necessarily tell her anything about the particular individual with whom she was working — such is the nature of research evidence.

One of the things which the writer has found himself doing in response to failure is to begin a systematic attempt to find out what he is doing correctly. It is far too sloppy to regard counselling as some kind of magical activity involving a near mystical relationship between client and counsellor which cannot possibly be described in anything but divine language. That sensuous view of the activity is perfectly adequate while work is going well, but as soon as repeated failure begins to occur, that counsellor is like a stranded whale. A very good analogy is with the teacher of physical education who often finds teaching a rather easy activity in early years; indeed, he or she can be quite a charismatic figure whose very presence commands respect and whose obvious physical ability is sufficient to determine the successful progress of lessons. When that teacher ages, however, success can diminish. If he or she has not learned the factors which contribute to success then stress and early retirement beckon. So too with the counsellor, whose practice can also meet with diminishing success as her freshness and vibrancy are dulled with experience. At moments of crisis it is not sufficient for the counsellor to have a general faith in herself, though that is important; it also helps if she knows the things which she does correctly. Obviously the details of these right-doings will vary from approach to approach, though it may be surprising to find the degree of similarity in the views of experienced practitioners of different disciplines. It would for instance be interesting to compare how practitioners from all fields viewed the importance of the following questions:

— Am I still able to meet each client as a totally *new* individual?
— Are my theories and my knowledge about human behaviour useful in helping me feel confident about understanding the range of human behaviour, or are they tending to make me blasé about people?
— When I attend to the client do I do that in such a way that they really see that quality and intensity of attention?
— In what ways do I communicate my commitment to clients?
— What qualities in me have been important for clients in the past and how might these change as I grow older and become more experienced?

There is one final thing which the counsellor can do in response to the experience of failure with a client, and that is to *use* that experience in work with the client. This seeming paradox is so important that it deserves a separate section.

The Therapeutic Use of Failure

Counselling is a relationship in which every facet of that relating can and should be used therapeutically. In the psychodynamic approach the client's transference of feelings and reactions on to the therapist creates many difficult and confronting situations which the worker will regard as therapeutic opportunities. In the person-centred mode the counsellor's ability to be congruent and use herself fully in the real relationship with the client is regarded as the cornerstone of the approach (Mearns and Thorne, 1988). Hence, every crisis in the therapeutic relationship carries a potential opportunity for therapeutic progress. This even applies to many of those situations in which the counsellor might simultaneously experience feelings of failure. If the counsellor can tolerate the difficulties of her own feeling and grasp those opportunities to engage the client then quite astounding progress can be made. Thus, for example, it is quite a common pattern for the client with low self-esteem to appear to make progress for a time and then to regress quite dramatically. This pattern of 'nearly succeeding' can recapitulate itself throughout all areas of his life and relationships including counselling. If this client were suddenly to declare the process a failure it would be the counsellor's responsibility to respect that perspective but not necessarily to collude with it. She would want to offer the opportunity to consider it carefully and to explore all the tracks that lead to and from this position. The danger in this example is that the counsellor will feel too threatened by the implied negative evaluation of her work and will not be able to continue functioning therapeutically. Instead, she will accept the client's definition of the situation and not seek to probe further lest she be made to feel even more uncomfortable. So this client leaves yet another failed helping process and the self-fulfilling prophecy of failure is further nourished.

Although the counsellor would want to explore the therapeutic possibilities in cases where the client cries 'failure', it is crucial that the worker accepts the possibility that the client's view *may* be more accurate than her own. This last point is important, for there is nothing more tyrannical in the profession than the counsellor who believes that any failing process is necessarily a function of the client's pathology, hence obviating any necessity for the worker to ask questions about her own way of being as a counsellor in relation to clients. Such tyranny appears to be behind many of the clients' experiences of failure described by Dinnage (1988).

Some of the more experienced counsellors and therapists in our research sample commented on this *therapeutic use of failure*; for example:

> When I heard my client hinting at failure I used to sink into the deep recesses of my chair, but nowadays I am pleased to say that I sit up and wait with anticipation to see which of us is going to learn most from this important confrontation. Perhaps it will be my client who learns about a pattern of relating in his life, or maybe it will be me who discovers something else about my functioning as a counsellor. If we can stand the pain then one or both of us is going to get something out of it.

Another experienced counsellor spoke about the importance of working with apparent failure but expressed frustration at her inability to do so:

> I'm getting really sick of myself not being able to get over this, but every time I hear 'failure' coming from my client I am disempowered — I shrink away from him and put up my defences. I can see myself doing that while actively knowing that I should be working with what is happening. It goes back to echoes from my childhood which scream 'failure' to me so loudly that I am still not able to rise above them.

If the question of failure is arising while the client is still in contact with the counsellor then exploration of it is possible, but even if the client has 'disappeared' the counsellor still has options:

> I have observed that it is important for me to reflect on such failures as quickly as possible with a colleague or supervisor in order to determine whether or not to take action. In almost all cases now I actually write to clients whom I have 'lost' in this way in order to make it easy for them to

return if they want to chance it again — or, indeed, to feel comfortable about withdrawing if that is what they truly wish to do. In about 60 per cent of cases they *do* return and the 'failure' usually then becomes the material for further progress.

When the counsellor is aware that failure is an appropriate word for what is happening in the counselling and that she has contributed to this state of affairs, great demands are placed on her professionalism which becomes focussed on the question 'Can I try to clarify *my* part of this mess so that we might at least have the possibility of moving on?' This question is a logical precursor to any 'therapeutic use of failure'. The opposite strategy, where the counsellor hides behind her greater power, disclosing none of her confusion and responsibility, is the kind of behaviour which is likely to mystify the vulnerable client and confirm his fears that he is bad or insane.

One of the therapists in our investigation described a case where he faced this crisis, but was able to *use* the feeling of failure:

> The client and I got down into a very deep level of work and then found that somehow her deepest self had some kind of antagonism or experience of threat from my deepest self. I went to my own therapist saying that I felt really despairing about it, and unable to continue. I felt as if I were touching bottom. If there was this deep rift, how could the therapy continue?
>
> My therapist brought out the ways in which this was a repeat of my inability to reach my mother and also my ex-wife. She encouraged me, I felt, to continue with this client.
>
> What I did was to tell my client about my despair and my inability to handle it. Her first response was to feel rejected, as if I had said to her that she was unacceptable and that I did not want to work with her any more. But as we went on talking it seemed as if there was some spark of something still there.
>
> There were other difficulties later, but we seemed to get over them more easily *because [emphasis added]* of that very deep moment of failure. At present we are doing some good work together.

At the beginning of this chapter we left Ann's counsellor in a state of despair, but this was not the end of the matter. With her powerful outburst Ann had made it impossible for the counsellor to avoid the painful question of whether he was indeed becoming 'the detached counsellor' — a technician who had developed the skills to work with clients while keeping his feelings well out of it. In some helping professions such a detached relationship would be regarded as acceptable, but for this counsellor it represented a much less powerful way of working. The shock of this incident led the counsellor to re-evaluate much of his current work, and to arrest his drift.

He also felt that his professional responsibility to Ann meant that a letter was appropriate. This letter openly described the counsellor's reactions to Ann's challenge and acknowledged his agreement with her criticism. It offered an appointment at the same time the following week should Ann want to explore things further.

The day *after* that next appointment Ann 'phoned to say that she could not make it the previous day, but that she would like to come at the same time the following week.

That meeting was begun by the counsellor giving as much detail as he could on all his reactions to their last encounter and earlier sessions. This time taken by the counsellor at the beginning of a session reversed normal practice where the counsellor is usually concerned to attend to whatever is uppermost for the client. However, in this case, it was most important for the counsellor to respond to the challenge which Ann had made at the end of her previous meeting.

Just as was noted by one of the practitioners mentioned earlier in this section, this experience of failure seemed to help Ann and her counsellor to get over later difficulties more easily. The two had been through a dramatic crisis in their relationship and both of them had shown an ability to *fight for the relationship*. This experience in itself proved of enormous therapeutic benefit for Ann who reflected upon it thus:

> When I stormed out that day there was no way that I was ever going to go back. I had cut him off and that was that — he was dead as far as I was concerned. The whole of that next week I buried him deeper and deeper by constantly re-playing the incident in my mind. Then I was astounded to get his letter and to read its contents. For the next few days I alternated between feelings of rejection towards him and thoughts that we might continue. I opted uncertainly for the latter and it became the first time in my life that I had ever really fought for a relationship. However, I wasn't going to let him off the hook entirely so I missed the next appointment intentionally!

Note

1. The 'Zeigarnik Effect' denotes the tension that is experienced when we are prevented from finishing a task and how that tension is sometimes reduced by fantasising what would have happened if we had been able to continue (Zeigarnik, 1927).

8 The Counsellor's Experience of Success

Dave Mearns

A Success

'You can go now', said Edward, 'I'm going to make it OK.'

Edward was in that heightened state of awareness where he could only speak the truth. Silently, I gathered my things together and left him staring out of the window of his flat. Three floors down I breathed the dawn air deeply. It smelt different, as though it were full of stimulants, but the intoxication was really coming from within me. I had spent the last six hours with Edward while he went 'cold turkey' with his life. Looking back at it across years of experience I suppose it is obvious that Edward was going to survive from the moment he had decided to 'phone me. In fact, I imagine that he would have 'made it' even if I had not met his request to visit him. But, leaving his place that morning, all I knew was that my work with him had been 'successful': not for the reason that he was now choosing life, but because he had faced that most fundamental question of whether he wanted his life. For about twenty minutes I felt a simultaneous exuberation and serenity which is difficult to match in human experience, until I was drenched by the cold realisation that somehow I had to stay awake to give four lectures that day!

What is Success?

Counsellors can strain themselves intellectually in their attempts to define 'success', though at a feeling level the judgement can be easy to make. For instance, the counsellor may feel positive about the process that is unfolding, yet would find it difficult to describe where this is going to lead the client. Similarly, the worker may *feel* uneasy about what is happening in counselling before her intellect can pinpoint what is wrong.

This chapter endeavours to tease out the experience of success with the help of questionnaire returns on the subject from forty-eight practising counsellors and therapists. The questionnaire was sent to seventy workers mainly from the person-centred and psycho-dynamic traditions. Since many of these had taken part in the earlier investigation of views on 'failure' (Chapter 7), a courtesy copy of that chapter was enclosed with the questionnaire. Though this was not a full-scale research project, it was felt important to comply with one of the central principles of 'new-paradigm' research in considering the research participants as respected collaborators (for an analysis of one such methodology applied to research see Mearns and McLeod, 1984).

The questionnaire was prefaced with the following:

> There is considerable research into *success* in counselling and psychotherapy. This is usually called *outcome research* and endeavours to evaluate the effectiveness of the process. Traditionally, outcome research has been regarded with a measure of scepticism and disdain by practitioners and trainees because it rarely addresses the lived *experience* of doing counselling or therapy. In the two open-ended questions which follow, I hope that you might let me glimpse your own experience of success without any need to justify that label.

There followed two open-ended questions:

1 Would you describe your *experience* of one significant success you have had as a counsellor/therapist? Does that success continue to influence you in any ways?
2 What other comments would you like to make on the *experience of success* for you as a counsellor/therapist?

As in the previous investigation of the experience of failure, no attempt will be made to do a quantitative analysis of the responses to these open-ended questions. They are designed to yield *qualitative* information on practitioners' experience.

Several respondents commented on their surprise that it was more difficult to focus on 'success' than 'failure'; for example:

> I found it a most useful yet quite taxing process to face myself with the question of *success*. It was easy to look at failures and even to begin to feel a bit better about them, but to take a cold hard look at cases I would call a *success* ran the risk of re-evaluating them as well!

Success may be the logical opposite to failure, but it is clear from the investigation that the *experience* of success is not a mirror to the experience of failure. Though there were exceptions which will be mentioned in this chapter, the experience of success was not such a dramatic event as that of failure. More often it was portrayed as a slow, steady movement, perhaps with occasional hiccups, but generally progressing in a quiet way, whereas failure is seldom steady and progressive.

Some counsellors have achieved that rationality of emotion which allows them to experience success and failure with equal intensity, but others appear to lose more through failure than they gain from success, for example:

— One of the things I have realised in looking at this question of success is that I don't really give myself the credit I should for the majority of my successes. One or two have been so clear and striking that I do derive a lot from them, but the majority I have largey ignored.

— I suppose, like many others, I'm always cautious about using the terms success and failure — and in particular 'success'. Somehow or other failure always seems to be clearer, whereas success is in some ways so seductive that I tend to look at it obliquely rather than face on.

A Successful Product

Where counsellors wrote of successful 'products' of counselling, they made *no* references to static features like the clients becoming 'happier', 'more contented', 'settled in their relationships' or 'emotionally stable'. Instead, their references were to clients achieving *dynamic* qualities which would enable their lives to change rather than stabilise, for example: 'She was no longer driven by her past' and 'He was now able to take charge of his own future development.'

This view of a successful ending as being a beginning of further change does not fit with conventional judgements of successful counselling. I recall the incredulity expressed by the wife of one of my clients in a 'phone call. She genuinely could not understand how the changes which had taken place in her husband could possibly be viewed as 'success'. She had seen her husband change from being a quiet, supportive, though mildly depressed man to one who was quite 'frightening'. He was more 'argumentative' and 'angry'; he 'cried a lot'; he 'spent more time on his own' and 'neglected his family duties'. In this woman's view the children were also 'upset by these changes in their father'. Each of these changes was a 'product' of the client's work in counselling. It seemed incomprehensible to his intelligent wife that anyone could conceive that these represented 'success'. And yet, viewed from the frame of reference of the client himself, he was now a man who was 'free from being governed solely by guilt'; 'able to risk showing emotions for the first time in my life' and 'more able to love my wife and children because that is something I now have a *choice* to do rather than *have to* do'. As soon as we adopt a wider frame of reference by which to judge the success or otherwise of the products of counselling we run into difficulty with value judgements. Some of the respondents to our questionnaire commented on this; for example: 'Doing therapy teaches me to take each person as an individual and not let the world's definitions get too much in the way.'

The Counselling Fairy-tale

There are times when counselling is strikingly successful in helping people to make dramatic changes in their lives. However, a more common consequence is that a period in counselling helps the client to gather knowledge about his own psychological processes and develop his social and emotional skills. The idea that counselling or therapy regularly revolutionises the person's life is largely a fairy-tale — a fairy-tale spawned of the anecdotes passed on by clients and counsellors and a fairy-tale reinforced by books like this which almost inevitably focus on the more dramatic experiences.

When we view the situation logically we should not be surprised that counselling is less potent than we imagined. A lengthy counselling contract might be an hour a week over a year or perhaps two years. This represents fifty or a hundred hours which endeavour to unravel and change patterns which the person has evolved and struggled to reinforce through perhaps forty years of living. Our fifty or a hundred hours is a drop in the ocean. We hope that it will be enough to help a change to *begin* and we should regard it as a bonus if the impact is huge.

Fairy-tales are the bane of a counsellor's working life. We see them mirrored so often in the neuroses of clients whose concept of life is that it should conform to the fairy-tales. But fairy-tales are tempting food for all of us, so the counsellor must similarly beware lest she falls into the trap of assuming that her work with clients must have fairy-tale endings.

Most often counselling is successful because of the other work the client is able to do in his life. Regular counselling sessions become an opportunity for the client to monitor, review and gain some new insights. As one of the respondents to our questionnaire said: 'Sometimes I am surprised when the client reports a gain from counselling when I haven't felt particularly "helpful". . . . This emphasises the fact that the role played by outside factors is usually greater than "me" in producing change.' This importance of outside factors is an obvious point, but one which is nevertheless important for the counsellor to consider while evaluating her work. I remember one client, Andrew, for whom the counselling hour represented the only laboratory in which he could experiment with a changing self. The following is taken from my reflections after our sixth meeting:

> After six sessions with Andrew I have realised that, outside himself, I am the *only* stimulus for change in his life. Although highly motivated, Andrew never knows where he wishes to begin at the start of each session. Usually a client wants to start with something that has happened

in his life since our last meeting. The interaction between the work we are doing in counselling and his life experience uncovers more facets to attend to. But with Andrew these outside factors are playing no part at all so far. In our meetings he is becoming aware of the patterns formed early in his life and also his feelings are more accessible to him. Normally, I would expect changes like these to interact with his outside life, particularly in his relationship with his wife. But it seems that all the facets in his life are so rigidly structured and programmed that nothing new is allowed to happen.

The counselling fairy-tale creates the expectation that the process will have magical results, but the reality of most counselling contracts is that the work interacts with the client's life to create small changes which the client can further develop. To focus too much on 'successful products' as a criterion of counselling effectiveness is to misjudge the power of counselling alone in the client's life. Counselling helps the client to develop new *processes* rather than steering him towards particular products. Indeed, regarding 'success' in terms of the products can detract from the counsellor's ability to function fully in the process; as one of our counsellors wrote:

> I know now that if I seek the 'experience of success' with a client I am more than likely to fail. Success seems rather to come from a willingness to accept and to be with what is — both in my client and in myself. Striving for results seems almost always to be counter-productive for it diverts attention from the flow of experiencing both with me and between us. I am at the point where I would submit that it is crucial to the therapeutic enterprise that a counsellor forgets all about success if he is to have the slightest chance of meeting his client at the level and in the manner that leads to hope and renewed purpose. To be 'hooked into' a need for success is to collude with the insidious forces of a vicious competitiveness and comparative judgement which nourish in our lives the very feelings of inadequacy and self-negation which bring many clients to the counsellor's door in the first instance.

A Successful Process

A conclusion from the above arguments is that while it can be relevant to examine the products created by the interaction of counselling in the client's life experience at the end of the counselling process, it can be disruptive to focus too much on products while counselling is in progress, except to the degree that these products claim the attention of the client. In evaluating their ongoing work the counsellors in our sample (mainly person-centred and psychodynamic in orientation) preferred to consider 'success' in terms of the processes which are happening; for example:

— The client was now able to trust me enough to bring out some of the things he was really scared of.

— For the first time he [the client] was able to confront me openly rather than shrink away in silence.
— It has been a long slow beginning but I think he [the client] is beginning to believe that someone (me) really does care for him.

When a counselling process is ongoing the counsellor has no idea what the eventual products are going to be, so the only meaningful way of judging success is in terms of how far the process seems to match what her training and experience suggest is likely to be therapeutic. This is similar to the procedure by which a psychologist judges the 'construct' validity of a test element. He matches the meaning of that element against others which he knows from his experience are valid. The procedure which the counsellor uses to judge the success of ongoing work is no less scientific nor human than that of the psychologist.

Sometimes this kind of ongoing evaluation by the counsellor is referred to as her using her 'belief in the process'. In many ways this is an unfortunate term because the word 'belief' connotes a kind of blind, mindless, unscientific following, while in actual fact the counsellor is setting and testing a series of sophisticated hypotheses — for example, two such hypotheses might be:

1 He [the client] has been pretty violent in his verbal rejection of me in the past few sessions, and yet he has arrived promptly for every appointment. Perhaps at some level he really wants help and it is important that I endure this barrage of his.
2 We seem to have been kind of 'stuck' for the last couple of sessions but perhaps that stuckness is appropriate for him [the client] after the big changes he has been making. Perhaps it's OK just to see what happens rather than try to push him out of his stuckness at this time.

Counsellors point to a number of factors which can indicate that a successful process is ongoing. John Rowan (1989), for instance, speaks about the point when therapy *takes*:

> One of the ways in which I recognise that success is on the way is when the therapy *takes*, in the sense that the person starts talking about how they thought more about what happened in the last session, or about how they have been recording their dreams and trying to work them out, or how they have been having insights between sessions. If this happens, it really seems to mean that success is on the way, and conversely.

Our questionnaire respondents mention other indicators of a successful process:

— Success for me is often about both the client and myself losing *fear*.
— Success is an increasing awareness of *equality* with my client.

— Success was feeling my client take back the strength which she had projected on to me for so long.

By perceiving small indicators such as these the counsellor may appreciate that a successful process is taking place before that fact is apparent to the client. I like to borrow the term 'osmosis' from biology to describe the imperceptible way in which the client absorbs elements of change. The client may not be aware of this gradual change until he realises that he is different. Counsellors report many examples of clients noticing that a change has taken place in them although they did not realise it was happening. As one of the participants in our investigation noted:

> I remember one client saying that she was out shopping one day, and walked up twelve steps, and on the top step she had a sudden thought — 'Happiness is a choice.' She realised that she had been assuming that happiness was not for her, and that she didn't have to assume that any more. It was a remarkable moment for her, and when she told me about it, for me too.

With some clients the counsellor's ongoing judgements about the validity of the process are sorely tested. The best examples of this come from those categories of client like the so-called 'psychotic' or the 'personality disordered' who are sometimes deemed to be 'inappropriate for counselling'. That phrase 'inappropriate for counselling' usually means the kind of counselling which institutions are prepared to subsidise. A mildly neurotic client who can still function quite well in the world may cope quite nicely with an hour a week in the counsellor's office. If that is all counselling is, then it certainly would not be effective with more severely disturbed clients. However, as I shall examine in a later section in this chapter, counselling can potentially be a much more flexible and committed process. The following extract is taken from the counsellor's notes on his work with a patient whose diagnosis was 'character disordered' — a rather old-fashioned term denoting a personality which was borderline psychopathic. In this extract the counsellor is struggling to make judgements about the process in the face of increasingly anti-social behaviour on the part of the adolescent client:

> It is a constant battle with Jimmy. That is to say: *he* does the battling and I make a point of not fighting him back; he tries to get me to reject him, and I don't; he tries to get me into the kind of relationship with which he is familiar, a fighting one. I think that deep down he wants the contact otherwise he wouldn't engage with me at all. Today he asked me where I lived, but that is the kind of thing I can't give him. I told him that I wasn't

going to tell him because I was afraid of the possibility he might damage my home. He said that that wasn't a very trusting thing for me to say, and I replied that he was right — I didn't trust him yet.

   With most clients, winning their trust is an initial step in the process, but with Jimmy winning his trust is what it is all about. It is crucial that I remain absolutely 'straight' with him. If I can do that and outlast his violence then we have at least the best chance of success, though even then he might withdraw.

If the effectiveness of this counsellor's work with the client were simply to have been judged in terms of its immediate products, then that client's deteriorating behaviour would certainly have been enough to conclude that counselling was not effective. However, that product of counselling was properly viewed by the counsellor as part of the process whereby the client was testing the counsellor's commitment to him.

Feelings of Success

The questionnaire asked counsellors to focus upon their experience of 'one significant success'. There was great similarity in the kind of feelings people described, for instance: 'exhilaration'; 'tingling'; 'intensely satisfied'; 'I felt like crying.' Another counsellor writes:

   Success is saying goodbye to a woman I have worked with for more than a year. Sounds crazy, doesn't it. We've laughed together, we've cried together, she's been in the depths of despair and the cauldron of confusion many times and I have tried to stay right there with her. I love her dearly.

Another describes the experience of success within one counselling session by means of an extended metaphor:

   My client comes in often tensed — at the edge of his chair — like a racehorse at the start of a steeplechase. He's suddenly off at the gallop — me alongside — adrenalin, awe, shock, wonder, flowing — then suddenly ahead a tricky water jump — potential for soaring on and ahead or sudden disaster. We're in the mud and water in a heap — struggling to stumble up and on or just up. Covered in mud and abrasions. We saw the danger but didn't rein in — that feels like a success!

Another counsellor ends his description of a key case thus:

   Jane is one of the clients who is very special to me. We are extremely close and we trust each other very much. We both recognise and value the other's integrity. I feel privileged to know her and to be so close to her. This closeness, valuing and respecting is a part of my experience of the success. It is a joy to know how much I have been able to help her. I do believe I did it, yet another part of me can't believe it. . . . What do you say when someone tells you that you have saved their life? I feel humbled by that. There is disbelief for me too. As Jane herself says, and

I completely agree, 'Can you save someone's life and effect so much change by just talking to them?' Somehow, together, we did it. Neither of us can believe it, yet it happened.

The experience of failure was sharpened in cases where the counsellor felt she had made a big *investment* (see Chapter 7) and exactly the same seems to apply in the event of success. In virtually all the key cases described by counsellors they had made a significant personal investment, usually stretching their own boundaries beyond previous limits to engage a client whose needs seemed at times to be too great. Another common feature of these descriptions was the degree of *intimacy* between client and counsellor. Indeed, some of the descriptions seemed to equate success and intimacy; as one counsellor reflected: 'Such caring, such willingness simply to be fully in each other's presence, always led to creative movement in the end.'

There is a marked similarity in these feelings of success even from workers of different counselling orientations like Gestalt, psychodynamic and person-centred. The accounts correspond very closely to Maslow's descriptions of *peak experiences* (Maslow, 1968) and at times clearly reflect a sexual quality. Sexuality is a powerful dimension of human experiencing, so it should not be surprising that it can be engaged during such peak experiences. The counsellor's sexuality does not magically detach itself from her personality upon entering the counselling room: it is a part of the counselling experience for both counsellor and client, though it often goes unacknowledged. This places a great responsibility upon counsellors of all traditions to begin to acknowledge, understand and hopefully come to *trust* their sexuality. The burden of that responsibility must fall even heavier upon male counsellors for male sexuality is more often imbued with the very qualities of power and dominance which can be most abusive.

In the survey returns from counsellors the feelings of intimacy which are mentioned appear to be very similar, but they are described by different words, including 'sexuality', 'sensuality', 'physicality', and even 'spirituality'. Perhaps these experiences are all similar, but understood by people in different ways.

Most experiences of success are quite fleeting, but some of the peak experiences just described have lasting consequences for the counsellor, like the following three examples from our survey:

— That case has helped lay the foundation of me feeling basically OK as a counsellor.
— Sometimes, when I experience failure as a counsellor, it helps to remember Gillian [the client] lives and that her children are

likely to be more balanced than they would have been if I hadn't seen her.

— My 'success' in that relationship still continues to influence me in profound ways. It encourages me to be fully present with my client with *all* the facets of my nature, not to deny the contribution of my physical and sexual self to the therapeutic encounter, to acknowledge the value and importance of my spiritual experience and understanding where this is clearly relevant and to accept powerlessness as part of a process which can enrich intimacy.

I recall one early case which simultaneously afforded long-term support and threat. The case had been a remarkable 'success', with the client moving from his early dissociated state through three years of regressions, disintegration and eventual re-integration. That success proved a touchstone of reassurance during many later moments of disillusion and negativism. But as well as being that harbinger of comfort in difficult times, the fact that the case was such an important success brought with it an element of fear . . . suppose the client were to come back one day as disintegrated as ever!

Flexible Working towards Successful Counselling

Without doubt I am less innovative in my present counselling than in my early years of practice. A settled family life, comfortable counselling rooms and a fairly demanding professional timetable contribute to my relative inflexibility with respect to counselling contracts. This present life makes me reluctant to take on some of the more challenging commitments of earlier years, like contracting with a client to spend seven days with him in a cottage in the country while the client went in and out of his psychosis, or a similar 'residential' approach with another client who could not face his grief in normal day-to-day living, but needed the intensity of the seven-day period including a single session of ten hours' duration. For both these clients such intensive working certainly pre-empted a period of institutional care in which they would not have received such concerted therapeutic attention.

The regular counselling hour was not a successful formula for these clients. In an hour they were only beginning to become aware of their fears, far less 'face my devil', as one of them put it. The single hour is a counsellor convenience which fits many, but not all, clients. At other times an extended session of two or three hours might provide a context which helps the client to focus in a more relaxed and committed way. Indeed, the very fact that the counsellor is willing to make this extra investment might encourage the client's greater trust which is necessary to make such a commitment.

The counselling room can become a place of power for many clients, but that is not universal. Sometimes it is stifling and epitomises the very stuckness which the client feels. In these circumstances I am always glad that our rooms are beside a very quiet spacious park where walks can unlock more than words. Yet extending sessions and walking in the park represent only small examples of what may be called *flexible working*. Sometimes the client has places where he wants to go to work. On one occasion I went with a client to the house where she had been raised. Simply sitting in the car, looking at the house, helped the client to relive some of the tensions and express the feelings she had swallowed in her youth. Another powerful place is a graveyard. Graveyards are good places to say 'goodbye', to express anger or to forgive. Having seen the uses which clients discovered for gravestones I have changed the instructions in my 'will' from cremation to burial, so that my children will have a focus for unexpressed feelings. Schools can be potent places — indeed, any place where abuse has been experienced can be evocative. A visit to a convent school was the request of one client. However, that evoked more than expected when we were met by a silent girl of about twelve years of age whose 'hunted' expression intensified my client's anger and frustration.

In the person-centred approach, which is my own tradition, there is little concern with maintaining 'boundaries' except those of ethics and confidentiality. We want to work with the *real* relationship between the client and the counsellor. The more intense and diverse is the relationship then the more it can be used. Hence, the idea of being with the client in different contexts is quite fitting to the approach. However, some of these examples of flexible working would not fit a more traditional psychodynamic approach which seeks to keep the counsellor more hidden as a person.

Flexible working can mean being willing to be used, and sometimes even abused, by clients. At present, one of my colleagues is working with a new client who makes many appointments, three or four each week, but misses most of them. Also there are several 'phone calls from him each week. I know that my colleague will be working with all that, and I also respect the fact that she is flexible enough to sustain such challenging behaviour and not feel the need to become defensive.

Working in the client's home is not a good idea as a rule, but sometimes it is the only place to work. It is many years since I entered into a daily contract with a client, but one such was with a youth who would otherwise have been hospitalised. The referral came through his sister who knew that I had worked in this way in a hospital setting. The client, Allan, had essentially withdrawn from the world, or more specifically he had withdrawn from his parents, as it later emerged. He stayed permanently in his room and was more or less mute. The beginning of my work with Allan was complicated by the fact that the only place to meet him was in his room, which meant coming through his parents' house, and, of course, being paid by his parents. Anticipating that this would inevitably be a crucial issue which would mitigate against his trust of me I spoke about the arrangements, the difficulties and my own feelings about these. There was plenty of space for me to talk freely because he said absolutely nothing for the first fourteen days.

The regularity of my meetings was important in that kind of working. I arrived in his room at exactly 4.00 pm every day, seven days a week, and left at precisely 5.00 pm. Wherever I had finished the day before I would start the following day — I wanted to be a constant feature in his environment and one, probably the only one, who was principally concerned with attending to him. Even after Allan broke his silence he still contributed very little for some time, and much of my behaviour was concerned with endeavouring to empathise with him on the basis of scant evidence. These attempts were little more than guesses about what Allan was experiencing, but put tentatively they sometimes met with a response. During the first few sessions with Allan, the only thing which sustained me was the commitment that I had made at the outset. Before even accepting the referral I had thought carefully about the context I was entering and how hard it was likely to be. In working with Allan in those early stages it was important that my resolve and commitment to the process proved to be stronger than his fear, for had I withdrawn it might well have intensified his isolation. However, after those first few sessions there was never any real question of my withdrawing because the experience of working with a client in this way is quite unique, though difficult to describe. A client like Allan gives so little back that every tiny offering is experienced with magnified importance. Sitting with him day after day *doing* very little intensified my own experiencing and helped to create that magnification. Any outside observer would have had no idea about the intensity of the experience going on between Allan and myself. In our silence we got to know each other more surely than clouds of words customarily allow. All the time it was clear to me that our relationship was forming and developing. It felt as though this strange process actually *could not fail* to develop the trust necessary for further work. It was only a matter of time. After forty-seven days Allan agreed to change the place of our meetings to my territory. Although this was only the beginning of a lengthy contract I felt that in making this change to move out of his room we had already largely ensured the success of our work together: in John Rowan's parlance, the therapy had 'taken'.

Flexible working has possibilities of which we have not yet dreamed. It introduces so many new variables. Imagine what it means for the therapeutic relationship to work with the client for seven days in a Scottish country cottage, where there are 'formal' sessions for two hours in the morning, afternoon and evening. The rest of the time is spent cooking together, eating together, climbing hills together and even trying to catch fish together. There is no way in which the counsellor can hide in a context like that, and the space it affords the client is unique.

Except for the case of Allan, all the experiences mentioned in this section have arisen from the suggestions or requests of clients once they knew that it was possible to move out of the counselling room. In no case were these flexible working arrangements a result of the demands of the counsellor. Flexible working may afford freedom to the counsellor to be creative in the contexts and methods she uses, but freedom is not the licence for uncaring or unprofessional practice. The counsellor who is working in flexible ways is introducing additional variables into her practice and consequently has to give more consideration to what she is doing and the effects it is having. Clients are not objects to be played with using our new, ever-more-exciting games and manipulations. Therapy abounds with examples of such abuse. I shall never forget the rage I felt at an American Humanistic Psychology Convention in 1972 when I realised that many of those who were displaying their 'techniques' were more concerned with creating clever manipulations than responding to human need.

One example of inappropriate 'flexible working' is amusing in retrospect, though not at the time. It concerned a counsellor who sought my supervision on a 'difficulty' he was experiencing with a client. Together we listened to the tape of one of his sessions. This was difficult for me because it was in a foreign language but near the end of the session I distinctly heard the woman client propositioning him. I checked on this and sure enough that was what she was saying. I was quite shocked and my supervisee seemed pleased that I had spotted his difficulty. The surprising thing was that there was nothing that had been said in the session which seemed to lead up to the client's very clear proposition. I was puzzled and eventually I asked the counsellor to describe the *context* in which he was meeting the client. To this question his response was:

We meet on Saturday evenings at 10.00 pm in my single room flat. There is only one armchair so I usually sit in that and she sits on the bed. Our sessions are between two and three hours in length and at the end I always give her a full body massage. . .[!]

Summary

This chapter has been based on the experiences of success of about fifty counsellors and therapists mainly from the person-centred and psychodynamic traditions. Perhaps if there had been greater representation of cognitive-behavioural counsellors we would have found more emphasis on the importance of specific *products* of counselling. Where such products were mentioned by our respondents they tended to be 'dynamic' rather than 'static', with the client, for instance, 'beginning to take more responsibility for his life outside counselling'; 'becoming more able to show his feelings'; and 'becoming strong enough to initiate changes in his life and relationships'. In the approaches sampled it can be misleading to evaluate counselling solely in terms of its 'products' while the counselling is ongoing because there is not a straightforward linear relationship between time in counselling and 'improvement'. Hence the counsellor finds herself making inferences about the success of the venture on the basis of her experience of its *process*. Some of the process criteria used by counsellors include: 'Is the client showing more trust?'; 'Is the client becoming more open about his real fears?'; 'Is the client showing more strength in relation to the counsellor?'; 'Is the client taking more responsibility for what happens in counselling?'

The chapter also endeavours to challenge the 'fairy-tale' of counselling success which maintains the myth that counselling is solely responsible for huge and consistent changes in the client. A more common 'successful' consequence of counselling is that it helps the client to 'begin' to make changes, but that the progress of these depends in large part on the interaction between what happens in counselling and outside factors in the client's life.

In exploring the experience of counselling it was appropriate to look at the actual *feelings* which success aroused in the counsellor. It was clear that these were felt more intensely when the counsellor was more involved and indeed they might be 'peak experiences' for the counsellor, even involving her feelings around sexuality and spirituality. Also the counsellor retains longer-term benefits from clearly successful experiences which may build up into a bank of success which can help the counsellor feel more able to cope during later crises of confidence.

Finally, the chapter traces the notion of *flexible working towards successful counselling*, emphasising that clients may choose more powerfully evocative contexts for work than single-hour sessions in the counsellor's room. The examples mentioned included work with clients who would normally be regarded as 'unsuitable for counselling', but perhaps the reality is that counselling is a potentially more effective process which is often limited by the restricted contexts we choose as counsellors.

9 My Experience of Counselling Couples

Senga Blackie

'Thanks for being there. We could not have done it without you.' My counselling contact with a couple has come to an end and their simple statement of gratitude fills me with a confusion of feelings. Embarrassment because I am not too good at receiving thanks; pleasure from the knowledge that their relationship is more satisfying for both of them; pride in the fact that I have been useful and helpful to them; and a sense of awe at the positive influence I can bring to bear on a couple's relationship.

Most couples who seek counselling help have experienced a crisis or change with which they are not coping on their own. They feel hurt, angry, confused and disappointed. Their self-esteem is diminished. They come to counselling looking for answers, for ways to make sense of what is happening to them, and for comfort. I offer them the opportunity to talk about themselves and their situation, to make sense of what can seem nonsensical to them and to explore their feelings in a counselling relationship with me. This relationship is characterised by my respect for them as individuals and my respect for their relationship, no matter how disastrous it appears to be to them. I try to listen accurately to what they say and how they say it, and to communicate my thoughts and feelings clearly to them.

I offer them warmth and a non-judgmental attitude, both of which are important, since being in a relationship which is in crisis can be a cold and hostile experience, full of blame and bitter recriminations. I demonstrate my interest in them and their relationship, and a desire to get to know them better. Perhaps contact with me also offers them their last hope before separation and divorce.

The experience of participating in this kind of relationship can encourage and enable a couple to find new ways of relating to each other. They can discover a capacity to communicate more effectively, become more loving and able to confront any future difficulties in a more positive way.

In this chapter I will discuss two examples of couple counselling and my approach to the process of couple counselling in more detail, and I will finish by writing of love — where most couples begin. First, however, I would like to say something about my own background and development towards the philosophy from which I now work.

My Background

I am the eldest of five children born to a miner and full-time wife and mother in the late 1940s. During my childhood I began to realise how unhappy and troubled my parents were in their marriage. I remember a time, when I was about ten years old, that I tried to encourage them to sit down with each other and talk about what was wrong. They could not do it. The arguments, fights and huffs went on until, many years later, they separated.

As a child I had needed them to talk to each other, and that need came from feelings of fear, anger and insecurity. I also seemed to know that if they could talk, instead of shouting or withdrawing from each other, then there was at least a chance of happier times. What I did not understand, then, was that they had no experience of a relationship where a husband and wife sat down to talk through their problems. My mother's parents had frequently abused each other emotionally, verbally and sometimes physically; and my father was seven years old when his father died, leaving his mother with five children to bring up alone. Neither did my parents have a counsellor who could offer them an hour a week away from the pressures of a large family.

At the age of ten years, I had no understanding of the effects of family or social influences on a couple's relationship, or of the emotional and physical turmoil which can accompany a communication breakdown. I only knew the feelings of helplessness and frustration at the apparent impossibility of making them sit down and talk with each other. I can still experience those feelings when I work with couples who seem to find it impossible to talk to each other with any commitment to their relationship. At times like that, I need to remind myself that the couple I am with are not my parents.

The need for good, open communication and understanding was a lesson I carried into my own marriage, at the age of eighteen. After ten years of reasonable success, I decided that I would like to become a marriage-guidance counsellor.

My early counselling practice was concerned with helping couples to explore their past in relation to their present. I helped them to understand why they had married or decided to live together, and why their relationship was now in trouble. To be involved in couple counselling in those early years, I felt that I had to see both partners together and work to a goal and time scale predetermined by them.

At our first session, we would try to discover what the problem was, decide on a solution which would suit both of them, and determine the length of time it could take them to achieve their goal. I offered couples a structure within which they could work together. I also offered them the constraint of having to work *together* because I thought that that was the best way for them to progress in their relationship.

I gradually realised that this was not enough for some clients and not relevant to others. I had to examine whose needs were being met in the counselling room. I decided that if I wanted to be more open to what my clients needed from their counselling relationship with me, then I had to listen to them more carefully and not only offer them my way of making sense of their relationship. I became more concerned with facilitating communication between couples and trying to understand the sense they made of their relationships. I began a training course on the person-centred approach to counselling and psychotherapy and this, along with ten years' experience of voluntary and private-practice work, has helped me to develop more flexible and creative ways of working with couples.

The Counselling Experience

When I meet with a couple for our first counselling session, I expect to be confronted by two individuals in conflict, each with a repertoire of powerful emotions and a range of ways of expressing those emotions. I also expect to meet two people who have committed themselves to a relationship which does not seem to be working and where each of them needs their side of the story to be heard. They are likely to be at a critical point in their relationship and looking for change. This desire for change can be expressed as a wish or a demand that the other partner change: 'She should stop working. . . .'; 'If he stopped drinking, then everything would be fine. . . '; 'We were alright until the baby came along, now she has no time for me. . . .' I hear one partner talk about the need for the other to change and usually discover that a development in their relationship has resulted in one of them feeling left out or left behind. Feelings of resentment have not been aired openly; instead these are expressed as criticism which can lead to more resentment and a defensiveness in both partners.

I also meet couples where only one partner assumes the responsibility for their difficulties, and the other is happy to concur with this:

for example, the wife who presents herself as being sexually frigid and the husband who prefers to agree with her rather than explore his participation and possible lack of sensitivity as a lover. Seldom do I begin counselling with a couple who accept equal responsibility for their relationship, although this is something which most couples tend to work towards.

When a couple walk through the door of the counselling room, they carry with them the tension of their troubled relationship as well as the apprehension of coming to meet a counsellor for the first time. I welcome them into counselling by offering tea or coffee, time for us to look around the room and at each other, chat about the weather or the traffic, and gradually we begin to say 'hello'. They start to talk about their difficulties and I listen, always checking that what I am hearing is, in fact, what they are saying.

This first session is crucial if I am seeing a couple together. I need to be sensitive enough to *both* partners to enable each of them to feel that I have some understanding of their individual experience of their relationship. It is also important that I show that I *value* their relationship even though they are questioning its value. As one wife recently said at the end of a first session, 'Do you think we are worth your time and trouble?' To this I was able to answer, very firmly, 'Yes'.

If, by the end of our first counselling session, the clients feel that they have been understood, valued and offered some hope for their relationship, then we can begin to work out the counselling contract. We discuss when, and how often, we are going to meet, as well as how much it is going to cost. I am convinced that this initial process of negotiation creates a potential for change in relationship. It is likely to be the first time in their lives that they have talked in this way with each other or with anybody else. Many are hesitant and unsure. I try to be sensitive to this, and while opening a door to a new way of discussing relationships, I try not to push them through it.

The ensuing development of the counselling relationship is unique to each couple. I will now discuss two very different examples of couples with whom I have recently finished working. They all gave their permission for me to use some of their material, and the second couple gave me individual, detailed accounts of what the counselling experience meant for them and their relationship. Apart from that, the following accounts are based on memory prompted by notes.

Ann and Bob
Ann and Bob came to see me, as a couple, on three occasions. At

our first meeting Bob did most of the talking. He was soon to go abroad to work and he was afraid their relationship would not survive the separation. They were spending a lot of time arguing and these arguments were becoming more serious. Bob took most of the blame for this. He said he could be very critical of Ann and he would lose his temper very easily. When Ann retaliated he would withdraw, feeling angry, hurt and confused. As I listened to Bob I felt very warm towards him; I liked his no-nonsense approach. I listened to his feelings of being to blame and soon found that I was experiencing a compassion for him and an understanding which had much to do with recognising and identifying with his feelings. It made me think of my own childhood and my grandparents, who had enacted a similar pattern of criticism, attack and retreat.

As he talked more about what was happening to them, I discovered that Ann and Bob had been living together for a few years. They both had marriages which had ended in divorce and Ann had a daughter from her marriage. It became clear that Bob had complex and complicated feelings about committing himself to being a husband and father. He liked having a home and family but he was also attracted to the idea of being single with no relationship responsibilities. My reaction to this familiar sounding dilemma was a mixture of 'I have heard this before' and 'I know from personal experience how difficult that can be at times.'

At this first session Ann agreed with Bob that he was mostly to blame for their problems. As I listened to her it became clear that she was afraid that the relationship with Bob would deteriorate in the same way as her marriage. This fear prevented her from listening to Bob, hence she could not understand why he could be so angry and critical. In the absence of this understanding, all Ann could do was to blame Bob and believe that the relationship would work if only he could change his behaviour. As often transpires in relationship problems, it was her *fear* which was the key, at least to her part in the difficulties.

She said she felt defensive in the relationship, and in the session she became angry and critical, then burst into tears because she felt hurt and rejected. I was taken aback by the force of her feelings and the explosive way in which they had been released. The only action possible for me was to sit quietly with her until we had both recovered. Bob also sat quietly and because we were nearing the end of the session, I decided that the most I could offer Ann was my awareness of how hurt and rejected she felt.

I felt uneasy about closing the session at a point where Ann and Bob would be left with a lot of expressed, but unclarified, emotion. However, I wanted to keep to our time constraints and also to give a little time to discussion of our counselling contract. I told Ann and Bob about my discomfort. I believe it is important to be clear about my own feelings in relationship with clients — in doing that I am modelling a way of relating which I hope they will develop in their own relationship.

We agreed to continue working together. I liked both of them and I felt that I could be open with them. I thought that they were receptive to me and also willing to be honest with me. During the session there had been moments of humour as well as tears and explosions — I enjoy working with a couple where we can experience a range of emotion.

Ann and Bob felt that in the first session I had understood them and could offer them the support they needed at the moment. They decided that they needed to pay more attention to their arguments at home, and agreed to report back to me the following week.

In our second session, we continued to focus on the feelings they experienced before, during and after their arguments. As I listened to Bob, I felt he was comfortable with the way they were both behaving at home although the feelings themselves were not comfortable to experience. He agreed with my perception and began to talk about his childhood and early family life.

He had been brought up in a family and school environment where arguing and fighting were almost the only forms of communication. His mother had died when he was young, leaving his drunken father to bring up three sons. He cried as he recalled his mother's death and other childhood experiences. He realised that all the relationships in his life since that time had been characterised by aggression. He also began to make connections between losing his mother and losing Ann. He wondered if his inability to commit himself more fully as a partner to Ann was based on the fear of losing her.

Ann listened to Bob's story with amazement. He had never spoken about his childhood in this way before and she cried with him as he talked about his mother. I, too, felt tears welling up in me and I experienced a tremendous tenderness towards Bob as he spoke about his troubled feelings with us. I also felt very privileged to be with this couple as they shared the painful memories and found new ways of communicating with each other. By the end of the session, they both felt that they had a clearer understanding of some of the reasons behind Bob's behaviour, and they were determined to work together to try to change it. They decided they would take two weeks before our next meeting to test out for themselves how they could now cope with the arguments.

As they left, I vividly experienced the contrast between my

intimate emotional involvement with them in the previous hour and my non-involvement with them for the next two weeks. It reminded me of my experience of relating with my daughter who lives away from home. When we are together, the closeness is palpable but then we must part because we both have our own independent lives to lead. The transition is a painful one while I am going through it but it is ultimately liberating and joyful and creates the space for renewed intimacy at a later time.

During the next session, Ann and Bob continued to become more aware of their feelings towards each other and about their life together. Their work in the counselling room was reflected at home, and by the end of that third session, they felt that they could continue without counselling support.

I had mixed feelings at the end of my counselling relationship with Ann and Bob. I felt pleased because we had worked well together and they had achieved their aims in counselling. They had begun to manage their arguments in a positive way and both felt more secure about Bob going abroad to work. I also felt disappointed, because I suspected they had the potential to learn to communicate even more effectively and I wondered if they would manage such development on their own.

The case of Ann and Bob is one example of what can be achieved in a relatively limited period to help a couple change their experience of living with each other. I listened to them as individuals, and to the disharmony in their relationship. I asked them if what I was hearing was a true reflection of their experience. They felt understood by me, and recognised in that understanding a different way of communicating with each other. They were committed to their relationship from the beginning, and they worked together both inside and outside the counselling room.

Carol and David
My experience of counselling with Carol and David was very different. I was involved with them over a period of four years. I worked with Carol for the first two years, then with both of them for four sessions, and continued counselling each of them separately for the next eighteen months.

The first time I met Carol she spoke only of her awful husband and awful marriage until I asked her how she *felt* about it, whereupon she broke down and cried. She said that no one had ever before asked how she felt about anything. At the end of our first session she said she felt better for being able to talk and cry, and that she would like to come back. We decided to give her husband, David, an open invitation to join us whenever he wished; but from her description of him, I felt that there was little hope of him turning up.

Meanwhile, Carol and I worked together, for several months at a time, over the next two years. She spoke of her fear and anger when David was drinking and threatening physical abuse. She spoke of her childhood; the influence of her religious upbringing; her relationships with her children, family and friends; her sexuality; and always she spoke about David.

During this time I grew very fond of Carol, breaking all my previously perceived rules about not becoming emotionally involved with clients. I identified with much of her childhood experience and felt angry for both of us and protective of her. My early training had emphasised the importance of keeping my feelings out of the counselling relationship, so that is what I struggled to do. The effect of this, though, was to create an artificial distance between us which was uncomfortable for me and caused Carol to be angry at me and to call me 'the perfect counsellor . . . stuck up on her pedestal!'

This was a tremendous learning experience for me and a turning-point in my relationship with Carol. I came down from my pedestal and left my 'perfect-counsellor' role behind me. I recognised that I had been paying more attention to people who told me how I had to be as a counsellor than I had been paying to my client. I became much more open with Carol about my feelings and how I experienced her in our relationship. She felt relieved that her anger had been heard and that she had not been rejected by me because of it and our relationship became closer with a greater degree of 'mutuality' to it — both of us able to be open and genuine with each other.

As she became aware of her experience and feelings about herself and others, her self-esteem and self-confidence increased. She became less able to tolerate David's abusive behaviour.

Carol and I had worked together for almost two years before David made an appointment to see me. I felt apprehensive about meeting the man who continued to abuse himself with alcohol, and his wife and family with neglect and disrespect. I feared that I might react negatively towards him and therefore would not be able to work with him. However, when we met, he was very different from the man I had expected to meet. He was a quiet, shy man who felt that his life was a disaster area. He acted 'tough' but underneath felt very lost and lonely. I immediately responded positively to his feelings and the reality of his abusive behaviour assumed less significance for me.

He spoke about his excessive drinking and gambling, and his fear that his marriage would break up because of these. He thought it would be a good idea if Carol and he came together for counselling the next time to see if they could find a solution to their problems. I saw them as a couple for the next four sessions.

When we were all together Carol found that she could no longer avoid the reality of their marriage. She heard David say that he wanted to change but recognised that he had no intention of doing anything about it. She felt that any open communication between them was impossible, and began to recognise ways in which she colluded with his behaviour; for example, she would make it possible for him to have enough money for his drinking and gambling by denying herself any share of the family budget. She continued in a sexual relationship with him when he had been drinking and she felt full of hate for him and for herself. She continued to cook and clean while pretending to herself and everyone else that her marriage was not as bad as she knew it was.

Once she had ended the pretence and confronted the reality of their relationship, she decided to terminate it. She asked David to leave home. I felt relieved that she had taken this initiative because I was aware of the tension that was building in the counselling sessions and I knew that my recurring feelings of frustration at being involved in their dishonest communication would have to be aired. It is better to air such difficulties rather than collude with them. Raising such difficulties gives the couple the opportunity to explore new ways of relating, but any such confrontation always carries the risk that one of them will terminate the counselling relationship. Carol's decision to end the marriage relieved me of the need for action and David did leave home.

Throughout the subsequent crisis, I continued to counsel each of them individually. David confronted the reality and consequences of his behaviour, and Carol faced up to living on her own and bringing up two children. During this time I felt that I was a link between them and an important third person who provided both of them with consistency, warmth, individual support and a sense of stability in relationship with another. I was able to maintain an independent relationship with each of them. They both accepted my need for confidentiality and I did not feel the need to disclose to either of them what was happening with the other. I became increasingly fond of both of them, although my relationship with Carol was qualitatively different: we achieved an intimacy which David and I never did.

I sometimes found myself listening to two different accounts of the same event within the same week and felt frustrated on occasions when they did not seem able to speak to each other about their different feelings and perceptions. There were also times when

I could quite cheerfully have banged their heads together and told them to get on with it, but I usually recognised those feelings as coming from my own lack of patience and kept them to myself. To have intervened with my impatience at such a critical point in their relationship may have distracted them from the delicate business of repair and rebuilding.

After several months of total abstinence from alcohol and gambling, and with the additional support of Alcoholics Anonymous and his parents, David felt strong enough to ask Carol if she would take him back into the home and Carol agreed to a trial period of living together again. I continued working with them separately because they needed to talk about what was happening to them as individuals. David talked a lot about his feelings towards Carol and his reactions to her. He used the counselling time to make sense of his feelings and then tried to change his behaviour when he was with her. Carol struggled with her conflicting needs to be independent and to be in a permanent relationship. She began to study for entrance qualifications for university, with David's support.

There came a point when the trial basis of the relationship ended and they decided to commit themselves to a more permanent arrangement. They had survived the trauma of separation and had come together again in an attempt to create a different relationship in which they could respect themselves and each other as individuals yet also live together as a couple and a family, with understanding, acceptance, clear communication and care for each other.

I had been involved with Carol and David and their relationship for almost four years, during which time I had developed a relationship with Carol which had been very important to me both personally and professionally. The two years with David helped me confront my doubts about myself in relationship with a man who exhibited attitudes and behaviours which frightened me and made me angry. I felt very grateful to them for trusting me with so much of their intimate lives and pleased with myself for sticking with them through thick and thin. I also think that my experience with Carol and David illustrates how it is possible to work flexibly and productively with a couple. I am aware that many counsellors would shudder at the thought of working with one partner, the couple and then both individuals simultaneously.

My Approach to Couple Counselling

My way of counselling couples owes much to my belief that a couple knows best when to come for counselling, and once there, they know what they need to talk about. I had this belief tested with Ann and Bob and have no way of knowing whether I was right not to suggest that they continue counselling for longer because I believed that they could learn more about each other and therefore develop a more satisfying relationship. My belief was more successfully tested with Carol and David. They also gave me the opportunity to experience how couples build and test their ability to relate to each other in new ways by *trying it out on me first*.

Carol's relationships before she came into counselling had been characterised by criticism and conditional love — she was only loved if she abided by her parents' 'conditions'. As a child, brought up in a punitive family and Church environment, she felt that she had no control over her life and no rights in her relationships. I learned to relate to her as a woman who has a right to her own feelings, needs and desires in our relationship. She was able to be angry with me and I did not reject or attack her. She telephoned me late one night to say she needed to talk and I did not tell her to 'pull herself together and get on with it' — I listened. She discovered her sexuality and I did not say she was 'dirty' or get embarrassed and avoid the subject. I was with her as she transformed herself from the unattractive wife and mother who wore her hair cropped short, jeans and jumper all the time, to an attractive sexual woman with long, curly hair and flowing skirts. She had always felt afraid in her relationships with women before she met me and together we managed to create a context where she was able to relate freely with me, another woman.

The importance of discovering new ways of relating in a couple relationship is heightened when the husband embarks upon this with a woman counsellor. With David, I had to surmount his experience of an uncaring mother and a rejecting wife. He became able to display a range of emotions with me which he had been unable to express with them. The experience of being able to be vulnerable with me and admit to his fears and worries gave him the courage to share these with Carol.

He revealed his sexual secrets to me and I did not damn him for them. Consequently, these secrets became less powerful and he eventually shared them with Carol, who was then more able to understand his behaviour in their sexual relationship. They subsequently resolved some of their sexual difficulties and were able to achieve greater sexual satisfaction with each other.

Of most importance was the fact that they each learned to trust another human being to be loving with them and willingly to engage in an open relationship with them. As a result they learned to trust themselves and each other to be more open and honest in their own relationship. I have no doubt that if at any time I had betrayed either of their confidence to the other, this level of trust could not have been achieved.

The most distinctive feature of my approach is that *I regard the relationship between the partners as a unit in itself.* Hence I am working with two individuals *and* their relationship. I honour that relationship as well as each of them and trust that if I can create the right therapeutic climate then the relationship will flourish as well as the individual. This is person-centred counselling with the relationship as the focus. As well as offering the person-centred 'core conditions' of empathy, unconditional positive regard and genuineness to each of the partners, I am also offering these to their *relationship*. I am struggling to *understand* the relationship and in so doing I am helping them to understand it. I am willing to *value* their relationship and consequently they may rediscover its value for them. Also, even though it can be difficult and painful, I am willing to be *genuine* in my responses to their relationship, and in that way, authenticity may be breathed into it.

It is likely that their relationship was born in a spirit of love, even though it eventually became unhealthy for them. If I honour that relationship then they have the best chance of honouring it, even if they choose to separate. Honouring the relationship does not mean trying to keep people together: a successful process might equally result in the termination of the partnership, *but* I would hope that they have found an ability to communicate openly and honestly with each other as two separate individuals who once shared a significant relationship.

Counselling, Couples and Love

I have decided to end this chapter where most couples say their relationship began — with love. The words 'counselling', 'couples' and 'love' go together very well. Every couple with whom I have worked has spoken of love: romantic love; sexual love; family love; selfish and selfless love. I offer them counselling love.

When I began counselling, love was a word which clients used, but which did not seem to belong to the process of counselling. I did not equate my loving self with my counselling self. However, over the years, due to my contact with many clients and other counsellors, I have experienced an integration — to be a counsellor means to be loving. This is particularly important when working with couples who feel that their source of loving has been cut off or destroyed. To experience the gradual erosion and complete disappearance of love can be traumatic.

In my marriage, my own struggle has been about learning to love and be loved; and to move from an eighteen year old's feeling that I loved my partner so much that I would die if he were not in my life, to a realisation that love means caring more about what is right for him in his world, than what I need from him in mine.

My struggle in counselling is to love my clients and their relationship for who they are, not for who they would like to be, nor for how I would like them to be. I want to love the clients who fall in love with me, the clients who are defensive or manipulative and even the clients who decide not to work with me.

Loving my clients means sitting beside them, sometimes holding them in their anger, fear, frustration, disappointment, guilt and despair, and trusting that if they are able to experience those emotions with me, then there is a good chance that they will be able to live more easily with them when they are on their own. For a couple to share their relationship with me is an act of faith in me and in them. As they gradually reveal more and more of themselves to each other, they are doing it with love and trust that they will not be abused in their vulnerability.

Michael Da Costa (1985: 5), counsellor and poet, puts it thus:

love.
the one thing that has the power to endow all
the rest with meaning.
an
affirmation of being. of the self. of the
other. of life.
'life and love are inseparable.'
even in the deepest moments of despair.
helplessness. hopelessness.
it is ever present
it is the tool of awakening and it is at the
same time that which is awakened.
it is present no matter how deeply buried,
how critically denied.
how rejected. your love. mine. ever present.
ever flowing. . . .

10 What Might be Learned from These Experiences of Counselling in Action?

Dave Mearns and Windy Dryden

During the production of this book we canvassed the experiences of more than 100 people involved in therapeutic endeavours, whether they called themselves 'counsellors', 'therapists' or 'clients'. These various experiences are intended to stand on their own in the influence they may have on the reader. For instance, Laura Allen's experiences of her 'bullying' psychodynamic counsellor and 'ineffectual' person-centred counsellor certainly do not reflect the norms in either of these traditions; but her poignant observations of how it *felt* to be a client might cause (a) practitioners to reflect on their own practice, and (b) clients to reconsider any assumptions they might have had about the omnipotence of the counsellor.

We did not plan this book as a deductive piece of research concerned with setting hypotheses, investigating them and drawing conclusions. Instead, we sought to compile a book in which experiences could be explored to provide a stimulus to further study. This book can be used by practitioners to reflect upon their own work and by counsellor trainers with their trainees. To this end we wish to use this last chapter to bring together some of the issues which seem to us to have been most important to practitioners and clients throughout the book.

As mentioned in the Preface, most of these experiences have been in relation to psychodynamic or person-centred counselling, hence the consistent emphasis attached to the subtleties of the relationship between counsellor and client. However, much of what has been said is also likely to be thought provoking for practitioners from most other therapeutic disciplines.

We shall present these issues in the approximate order in which they are likely to occur in the kind of counselling process depicted by John McLeod in Chapter 1. First, the client and counsellor establish a *contract*, after which it is the qualities offered by the counsellor which seem to be most important to the client as he makes his decision about whether or not to step into the unknown.

The kind of qualities which seem to have been highlighted throughout the experiences mentioned in this book include the *transparency* of the counsellor, her *commitment*, her ability to *engage* the client and the *containment* she offers the client. These qualities contribute to develop an intense and apparently close working relationship, but a fascinating aspect of that relationship is just how much of it is not talked about between client and counsellor: we call this *the unspoken relationship*. Thereafter, we shall look at some of the issues which can follow upon the point when counselling becomes established and consider the interaction between experience in the counselling room and outside it whereby the *processes* which the client develops and practises with the counsellor can become useful *products* in his life outside. We shall also consider how that outside life can radically affect the process of counselling, before concluding the chapter with some observations on *endings* and suggestions on future *uses* of the experience of counselling.

Establishing a 'Contract'

One of the effects of producing this book has been to heighten our awareness of the importance of establishing a *clear* contract between client and counsellor at an early stage in the counselling process. Experienced practitioners have had many 'beginnings' and it is easy to forget how crucial this step can be for each new client. In Chapter 1, John McLeod summarised the evidence from Maluccio (1979) and Gaunt (1985) in suggesting that this early 'contract-forming' was crucial lest the client feel confused and rejected or assume that the counsellor was not interested in him. The experience of Myra Grierson (Chapter 3) provides a striking example of how important it is for the client to have clarity on the contract — to be really sure that this counsellor is making a commitment to her and will not suddenly discontinue the process. Myra describes her first counselling experience as one in which she had lived with the constant tension of the possibility of the contract being ended. In her second experience she showed understandable relief when the elements of the contract were formally explored in the early sessions.

However, contract-forming is not simply a matter of discussion in the first session — it needs repeated restatement and clarification. Clients are often too confused or vulnerable in the early sessions to be really sure about what is being offered, and some do not dare to believe that the counsellor's offer is real or enduring.

Implicit in the early exploration of a contract is the possibility that the client will be using these first sessions as a means of investigating and *selecting* a counsellor (see Chapter 1). It is generally regarded as good practice for a client to take an active role in choosing a counsellor whom they feel will be helpful to them, but the reality is that many clients are only just strong enough to approach *one* person. Laura Allen's description of her first counselling experience points to very bad counselling practice from the outset but she was trapped by her own lack of power until the last vestiges of her self-respect helped her to break free. There is no easy way for the counsellor to help a vulnerable client to assess the counsellor and make a choice. Even 'one-way reviews' whereby the client is encouraged after three or four sessions actively to ask the question 'Is this counsellor right for me?' run the risk of being misperceived by the client as a covert suggestion by the counsellor that they should stop working together. A more radical approach to this and other difficulties that the client may have in counselling is to set up a facility whereby clients can exchange views with each other. Many clients value the anonymity of the counselling experience above all else, but others would be interested in having available the possibility of entering a loosely structured network of clients and former clients who could make contact with each other to explore their experiences. Some counselling centres will, of course, offer such a facility in the form of counselling groups for current or former clients of individual counselling. An extension of this kind of thinking in the future might even lead to the existence of 'consumers associations' for clients. Anything which would serve as a challenge to the tyranny of 'therapeutic' practice as experienced by Laura Allen and many of the clients in Rosemary Dinnage's study (1988) should be welcomed by the profession.

Counsellor Qualities

In Chapter 1 John McLeod suggests that an early concern for clients, as evidenced in the research literature, is their evaluation of the counsellor in terms of the question, '*Is this a person who can help me?*' Much has been written on counsellors' views about the 'counsellor qualities' which are most important — for example, Rogers (1951) and Mearns and Thorne (1988) — but our 'client-experience' chapters written by Myra Grierson, Laura Allen, Brendan McLoughlin and Rosanne and Paul offer the client's perspective. From their accounts four qualities seem particularly important: *transparency*, *commitment*, *engagement* and *containment*.

The Transparency of the Counsellor

John McLeod quotes Timms and Blampied (1985) who suggest that the client begins to take more interest in the counsellor as a person towards the end of the counselling contract. However, for Myra Grierson, Brendan McLoughlin and Laura Allen it was important to their experience of the process to see behind the role of the counsellor to the 'person' underneath. For Laura Allen this transparency was a matter of survival in that it allowed her to judge that there was something very wrong with this man who was her counsellor. Brendan McLoughlin seems to have been just as influenced by the few glimpses he got of the person of his analyst than about much of the other work they did together. Indeed, this experience has considerably affected his own practice as a counsellor and therapist in that he recognises the importance of acknowledging and working with the 'real' relationship as well as the transference relationship. Myra Grierson gives us numerous examples of the importance to her of seeing through the role of the counsellor to the person who lay behind. With both her counsellors it was important for her to 'see his vulnerability'. This seemed to have a direct and immediate empowering effect for Myra who stopped investing all her faith in this now flawed person and began to realise that she 'had to be responsible for myself now'. The transparency of the counsellor was also important for Myra in her second counselling experience where the counsellor did not deny her suspicions that he was 'bored' and 'withholding'. By that stage in her own development Myra was quite sure about her judgements of this other person and if he had been anything less than transparent to her challenge she might well have lost confidence in him.

This quality of transparency in the counsellor seems to be quite subtle in its effects and has a lot to do with social power. While the counsellor stays hidden behind her role she attracts the inference of power which that behaviour denotes in our culture. However, when she becomes more transparent and allows the client to view her as a person she simultaneously loses some of that inferred social power but may gain in the power which ensues from the client's respect for her as a person. Putting this another way, the counsellor's transparency may lose her some power in the transference relationship but will gain it in the 'real' relationship.

The Commitment of the Counsellor

The power of the counsellor's commitment to the client is evidenced in most chapters in this book. The chapters on the counsellor's experiences of success and failure point to the counsellor's commitment in the form of her 'personal involvement' as being the most crucial determinant of the strength of the experience: the more the counsellor was committed then the more powerful was the experience of success or that of failure. This is taken even further in the section on 'flexible working' at the end of the chapter on the counsellor's experience of success. In his work with the mute client, Allan, Dave Mearns reported that on an experiential level commitment appeared to be not just a necessary but also a *sufficient* condition for success. Although it was fourteen days before Allan uttered a word and forty-seven days before he was willing to move out of his bedroom, the experience for the counsellor was that such a large commitment to the client could not fail to succeed in the end.

The importance of the counsellor's 'commitment to a process' with the client is exemplified in Brendan McLoughlin's 'rebirthing' experience where he felt enormously stimulated and then deserted. Indeed, in reading Brendan's writing there still appears to be a feeling of a process unfinished in relation to that rebirthing experience. However, that experience helped Brendan to appreci-ate how important it was for him as a counsellor and therapist not to desert his own clients but to offer them a commitment to the process which would see him being responsible to the client and what they created together, including all those difficult transference experi-ences which were never even acknowledged in his experience with the rebirthing therapist.

'Commitment' to Myra Grierson as a client was represented by the accessibility of her first counsellor. It was an enormous resource to her to know that her counsellor was committed enough to allow her to contact him in between sessions and indeed at intervals after their main counselling contact was over. As Myra observed, this kind of commitment on the part of the counsellor is generally not abused — the very fact that clients know that the counsellor is available to them often means that they do not need to get in touch.

Senga Blackie showed a huge commitment to Carol and David and their relationship, for she was working with them individually and together at different times. It is easy to see from this case-study how Senga's policy of being committed to the relationship as well as the two individuals can help the couple to rediscover the commit-ment to their relationship which they once had.

The Quality of Engagement Offered by the Counsellor
Counsellors vary in the quality of personal engagement they offer to clients. Some give the client the experience of being engaged as an unique individual, with the client feeling listened to without being

categorised or diagnosed. Although the 'engaging' counsellor is operating from a coherent theoretical frame of reference (Combs, 1989), that theory will not be experienced by the client as imposing treatment techniques to be employed with particular 'kinds' of client as if the uniqueness of the client was of little concern. The contrast is the counsellor who is experienced by the client as not engaging with him as an individual, but seeming intent on understanding his 'problem' in a diagnostic sense and applying the treatment which is 'appropriate' to that problem. The concept of engagement encompasses 'listening' as one of its major activities, but it is wider in that it implies a willingness to work within the frame of reference of the client rather than exclusively from the perspective of the counsellor. 'Engagement' is experienced quite powerfully by the client as the counsellor reaching out to him rather than staying more detached and simply working with his 'problem'.

Brendan McLoughlin gives us examples of contrasting experiences with respect to engagement. With his rebirthing therapist he felt that he was only a simple 'ingredient' while the therapist, who had not met him before, held the 'recipe' which was to be followed. On the other hand he experienced his analyst engaging with him where he was, rather than imposing interpretations. Laura Allen also observed that her first counsellor 'had his way of going about things regardless of who was in the other chair', while, from the counsellor's perspective, Senga Blackie recognised disengagement in herself when challenged by Carol to come down from her 'perfect-counsellor' pedestal. In summarising her experience with both counsellors Laura Allen felt that they were both in their own way 'inflexible' people who could only relate with her in quite a narrow way: neither could engage with her on her own terms.

Myra Grierson appreciated her second counsellor's quality of engagement when she realised, on her train ride, how he had patiently stayed with her 'track' even though there were 'too many words'. In doing this he had reached out to her more than her parents had ever done. Her long 'narratives' (Chapter 1 and Rennie 1985a) may have seemed wasteful of time but that was the way her 'tracks' worked.

The Containment Offered by the Counsellor

'Containment' is a basic sense of being 'held' and protected by the counselling relationship — being given utterly reliable safety and support. It involves the personal reliability of the counsellor but also the reliability and sufficiency of the counselling structure — for instance, a consistent place, time and duration of meetings. Brendan

McLoughlin was the only writer to use the concept of 'containment' but many of the other writers referred to the same experience. Myra Grierson, for instance, pointed to the stability and consistency of her second counsellor and contrasted that with the relative unpredictability in the structure of sessions with her first counsellor. Rosanne referred to her counsellor as a 'haven' and Laura Allen was quite clear how much she desperately needed to experience containment with her first counsellor when she said that she 'wanted to be held, not necessarily physically'. Indeed, Laura's sense of what she required during that early period of disintegration and abject fear is a powerful example of how fundamental the need for containment can be for clients who feel desperate. Brendan McLoughlin regards containment as a 'key concept' in his own practice, and it is difficult to see how anything could develop in counselling without the client feeling some measure of containment.

These terms *transparency*, *commitment*, *engagement* and *containment* seem to be the most descriptive of the important qualities upon which our writers commented. Not surprisingly they have their parallels in other theoretical terms. 'Transparency' has been used as an alternative for 'congruence' in person-centred theory while the concept of empathy seems to be an aspect of 'engagement'. Furthermore, the four qualities are by no means distinct. In particular, commitment, engagement and containment overlap, since both engagement and the client's experience of containment inevitably involve a high degree of commitment on the part of the counsellor.

Although these are qualities which seem to be important to counsellors and clients alike, they are seldom matters of discussion *between* the counsellor and client. One of the most fascinating paradoxes of counselling is that despite its appearance as a relationship of great openness, clients rarely air their most serious difficulties and troublesome questions about their relationships with their counsellors. These issues form the submerged part of the iceberg — the part we shall call *the unspoken relationship*.

The Unspoken Relationship

It is clear from the 'client' chapters in this book that there is a considerable amount of their own experiencing which clients do not disclose to their counsellors. In John McLeod's chapter on the client's experience he mentioned the research of Rennie (1985a), who observed that the client's 'narratives' were often serving the ulterior purpose of portraying the client in a favourable light. However, there are many more ways in which the client, and sometimes the counsellor, feeds the unspoken relationship between them. Rosanne and Paul both had several unspoken reactions to particular things their counsellor did and for some time Laura Allen conformed to Rennie's (1985b) finding that clients were reluctant to disclose their disenchantments with their counsellors. In Laura's case it is easy to understand her withholding on the grounds that she was particularly vulnerable and did not want to risk losing this counselling experience which she felt was her 'last hope'. She was placing a 'blind faith' in her counsellor in the belief that he knew best. In this context it is understandable that she subordinated her feelings about the counsellor. Indeed, the surprise in Laura's case is that she eventually *did* confront him rather than accepting his definition of her and progressing obediently to psychiatric hospital.

Probably more than any of the other writers, Myra Grierson allows us to glimpse these unspoken parts of her relationships with her counsellors. She tells us how she was scared to 'open up' in the early stages of her work with her second counsellor. She felt that if she was open about herself then she would look so horrible that the counsellor would reject her. However, she was also fighting against the inclination to try to please her counsellor by being an 'interesting client' because she knew that this would not really help the process. Myra feared asking this second counsellor how he experienced her long story-telling in case he confirmed her suspicions that he was bored, but she was so committed to the counselling process that she defied her fears and did not relegate that material to the unspoken relationship but voiced it. The dividend for her investment was that the boredom was not denied and far from destroying her it enhanced their work together. It is relatively rare for clients to do what Myra did and *initiate* work with the unspoken relationship. Usually these fears, confusions, ambivalences, suspicions and doubts about the counsellor or their work together are left unvoiced, partly through lack of confidence in working with such difficult material in relationship to a more powerful person and partly through fear of rejection or other punishing consequences of such confrontation. Perhaps counsellors forget just how much clients think about the counsellor and about how the counsellor experiences them. With this in mind, one of us (DM) has recently been experimenting with more frequent disclosure of his experiencing in relation to the client. As well as sometimes sparking off responses in the client this also seems to serve the purpose of correcting assumptions about the counsellor's experiencing which the client had already relegated to the unspoken relationship. Thus, for example, following a previous session when a male client disclosed a childhood incestuous experience with his father and uncle, the following dialogue took place:

> *Counsellor*: Throughout this session I have felt that you have been more distant with me than before. That has felt strange for me because I have been feeling especially close to you and aware of just how much you shared with me last week.
> *Client*: I've felt terrible today. . . . I wished I hadn't come. . . . I was wanting to run away and never see you again. I thought you were disgusted with me for what I did with my father and uncle.

The unspoken relationship is of course the potential source of considerable material that the client and counsellor can meaningfully use in their therapeutic work. It is the container of many of the client's assumptions, projections and identifications as well as the parallels of these in the counsellor. At various times the counsellor will endeavour to tap into that unspoken relationship to work with the material contained therein. However, the central questions which remain are: how much of the unspoken relationship is still kept hidden by the client? . . . and why?

When Counselling Becomes Established

If the client experiences the counsellor's qualities as 'good enough' and the unspoken relationship is not too inhibiting for the client, then he may choose to let go of his restraint and trust the counsellor and their work together. That choice is something about which we know very little. Myra Grierson's confrontation of her counsellor represented an extremely important commitment on her part, but what led her to make that commitment? Dave Mearns was confident that even Allan, the epitome of the withdrawn client, would eventually make that commitment, and after forty-seven days he did indeed agree to change their meeting place, a move which represented a considerable commitment on his part; but what actually prompted that change? This book can offer no explanation for that important moment in counselling when the client redefines the situation, but suggests that it is one specific area for future research.

After that commitment is made and counselling 'takes' (Rowan, 1989), the process changes quite considerably. It is interesting to note that in all the counsellor and client experiences recounted in this book, few have been devoted to this part of the counselling process. It seems that much more concern is experienced both by counsellors and clients about the earlier, 'beginning' phase of counselling. Once counselling becomes established a lot of important work can happen very quickly, but often without the same element of struggle and conflict which clients and counsellors experience in the early stages. The best account of this phase is given in the chapter by Rosanne and Paul. They even drew a curve to depict their experience of the whole process from 'opening' down to 'rock bottom' through 'resurfacing' to 'ending'. One of the remarkable features of their observations is that their sketch perfectly mirrors the so-called 'transition curve' as depicted, for instance, by Adams et al. (1976) and broadly supported by the observations of Kubler-Ross (1969) and Parkes (1972) with respect to the process of grieving. The 'transition curve' represents the way many people experience major life changes. The onset of the transition is followed by a plateau which gives way to a deepening depression, a later turning-point ('rock bottom') and a gradual 'resurfacing' to an end-point which is usually drawn higher than the beginning to depict the fact that successful completion of a transition can result in the person experiencing a *gain* in self-esteem or perceived emotional strength.

The curve which Paul and Rosanne draw at the end of their chapter exactly reflects the transition stages and reminds us that counselling is a process of change which can involve a downward movement as a natural part of that process. In other words, the experience of counselling can appear to make things *worse*, at least in the short term. Usually what is happening is that counselling is providing enough security for the client to experience the thoughts and feelings which are *really* difficult. Once the client has made the decision to invest further in the process and the counselling has become established, some of the client's safeguards and restraints are removed. In these circumstances, more sessions may appear to fit the 'heavy-going' and 'foundering' categories used by Orlinsky and Howard (1977) and described by John McLeod in Chapter 6. For the counsellor the experience can feel like one of 'getting lost with the client' in the sense that neither knows where they are going. At this time the client is entering his worst areas of darkness and unclarity with the strength and containment he derives from his relationship with the counsellor.

Process as Product

One of the themes which emerged in Chapter 8 on the counsellor's experience of success was that the distinction between counselling process and counselling product was often a spurious one because many of the processes evolved in counselling become 'products' of the counselling which the client can use in other areas of his life. In counselling, for example, the client will learn to engage in the process of *listening* to the underlying as well as the superficial feelings he has in relation to events in his life; he will become *aware* of some of the assumptions he makes about other people and how these influence his behaviour towards them; and by expressing rather than concealing his feelings he may become *less frightened* of his whole affective domain. These are just three common elements of counselling process which are likely in themselves to become products for the client in the sense that he can use them in his wider life experience.

There are numerous examples of this in the other chapters in the book. In Senga Blackie's work with couples, for instance, she mentions the use which the male client can make of his relationship with the woman counsellor. The development of this relationship between the male client and the woman counsellor is simultaneously an element of the counselling process *and* one of its 'products' to the extent that the man discovers new ways of relating to women, including his partner. Also, at the end of her chapter, Myra Grierson observes that she has come to 'value her chaos . . . because it is a sign that there is something going on inside of me which will eventually sort itself out and I will move towards a new clarity.' Even such an apparently negative experience as 'chaos' within the counselling process was retained by her as a useful product.

Brendan McLoughlin, also at the end of his chapter, reinforces the view that it is the processes which we practise in counselling which become the most useful products of the experience:

> The achievement of counselling is not that it stops us smoking, or takes our depression away, or makes us more confident. The achievement is that it helps us to be more responsive to ourselves as whole beings, mind and body, psyche and soma. If we gain the courage to face up to our conflicts and fears rather than avoid them or push them away into symptoms then we have made good use of counselling. . . .

Is There Life outside the Counselling Room?

Just as counselling processes can become products for the client's life outside the counselling room, so too does that life have a considerable and perhaps underestimated impact on the counselling process. John McLeod, in both Chapters 1 and 6, quotes the research of Maluccio (1979) in pointing out that it can be difficult for the counsellor, who only meets the client in the context of her office, to realise just how much of the changes which appear in the client are influenced by the rest of the client's life rather than by the counselling process. This might appear an obvious observation but it is one which is often missed from the perspective of the counsellor who only sees the client in the same context each week and naturally attributes change to what happens there. In Dave Mearns's chapter on the counsellor's experience of success (Chapter 8), this paramount importance of outside factors was stressed. In addition, it is interesting to compare Senga Blackie's work with her two couples. In the case of the first couple, Ann and Bob, there appeared to be considerable opportunities for their life outside the counselling room to have a large impact on the counselling process. However, in the early stages of work with the other couple, Carol and David, that life outside counselling seemed in fact to detract from gains experienced within the counselling room. In the one case counselling lasted only a few sessions while the other contract was measured in years. The difference is not only attributed to the influence of outside factors, but it is a major issue which counsellors frequently underestimate.

Endings

Part of the 'fairy-tale' view of life and counselling is that the 'ending' can only come once the client has completely changed his life and become 'happy-ever-after'. The classic fairy-tale ending would see the now fully functioning client disappearing into the sunset with a wave of farewell to the counsellor who is no longer needed. Now the former client is a free spirit who has found happiness, autonomy and reason for living. Never again will he need to seek the help and support of others in a counselling capacity — he is now his own counsellor.

As with all fairy-tales there are just enough fragments of reality in the above to make it believable. We would expect the client to become more free from fear, and more able to be autonomous. In addition, as Brendan McLoughlin describes in his chapter, we would expect the client to have developed the 'counsellor' part within himself, perhaps in the sense which Rosanne means when she says: 'The experience continues as part of an inner process long after the sessions are ended.' However, counselling does not change people's lives. The notion that the client's life should now be 'happy' or 'fulfilled' as a result of counselling is something which the counsellor just cannot offer. All counselling can do is to help the client to develop the 'tools' which he then might use to make changes in his life. These 'tools' might include his awareness of the influence upon him of earlier traumatic events, his understanding of his own self-defeating behaviour and his new-found ability to behave in alternative ways. The changes in his life which will result, far from being of the 'happy-ever-after' variety are more often doused with the cold water of reality — the client may realise that his life and relationships up to that point had their foundations laid in his 'neuroses', and that many frightening and painful changes to his life and those relationships will follow.

Expecting the fairy-tale ending gives a spurious and somewhat disabling notion of counselling. Counselling is not a process of going to an expert who will then heal the client so that he does not need that expert any more in the future. That image of counselling simply reflects the expectations we have of mainstream medicine. There is little likelihood that just sitting down and talking with someone for a number of hours would produce such permanent magic. A more accurate view of what counselling can offer is a context which the client can use to focus on himself and his life with skilled support and without distraction. The emphasis is not so much on the 'magic' the counsellor can perform but on the client being enabled to follow his own 'tracks' (see Chapter 1 and Rennie, 1984), and developing his own 'tools'.

It is quite common for endings to occur when the client has achieved only a portion of what he wants for himself in the longer term. In Chapter 7 on the counsellor's experience of failure, one client ended the counselling process when she became aware that the strength she was finding in herself might lead her to leave her marriage. At that time she judged that she was not yet ready to follow this track. Also, Myra Grierson's work in counselling was by no means finished at the end of the time with her first counsellor, but she had achieved 'enough' by that time. Though her process of personal development was only beginning at that ending, that first counselling experience had succeeded in 'saving her life'. In Chapter 4, Rosanne is clear that the ending came at a time when they had moved on 'a little'. Indeed, when Rosanne and Paul stopped they anticipated that they might start again at some later time but they had moved on 'enough' for their relationship at that time. Perhaps there is a lot to be investigated through research on this issue of endings. Thus, for instance, the hypothesis that a time for ending is the point at which clients feel that they have done 'enough' for now would be interesting to explore. If this is a significant issue for clients we might expect that continuation beyond this point, as often happens when people are expecting the fairy-tale ending, would result in relative 'stuckness' because in reality the client is not ready for more change at this time in his life.

The Uses of the Experience of Counselling

A recurrent theme in this chapter and in the book as a whole has been that of *communication* between client and counsellor about their experiences of the process and of each other. It is to this that we want to direct particular attention at the close of the book. The sort of questions which may be important for gaining an adequate understanding of the process of counselling include:

— How aware is the counsellor of the client's experience?
— How aware is the client of the counsellor's experience?
— How accurate are the assumptions the client is making about how the counsellor experiences him?
— How accurate are the counsellor's assumptions about how the client experiences her?

In Chapter 6 John McLeod suggested that questions such as these were important for future research in counselling, but it may also be fruitful to make more use of the products of these questions in ongoing counselling. One of the editors (DM) has published a case which was constructed jointly by the client and counsellor on the basis of questions such as these about each other's experience (Mearns and Thorne, 1988). Although that had been a 'successful' counselling experience, and the relationship between counsellor and client had been perceived by both as being strong, the process of exploring each other's experience of the process exposed many aspects of the hitherto 'unspoken relationship' which might have been a focus for important therapeutic work.

Perhaps one of the challenges for research and also counselling practice in the future is to discover ways of tapping the experiences of counsellor and client at many different levels. It may be exploration such as this which will allow other dimensions of the counselling experience to be brought into the realms of definition and understanding. For instance, might this be an avenue through which we could eventually understand the ethereal quality of *intuition*? What is the 'intuitive' worker actually *doing* when she is experiencing strong sensations and interpretations which prove to be accurate or useful? Certainly her empathic ability is involved, but she may also be making very fast deductions involving different levels of her own and the client's perspective, piecing together minute clues from things the client has said and from her experience of the client. Counsellors will often have the experience of 'sensing' consistencies and inconsistencies in the client before they are actually able to work these out and describe them. Perhaps, then, our 'intuition' is in part explained by our intellect: our ability to process information at immense speed from different perspectives and become aware of such consistencies and inconsistencies long before we can explain them.

Investigating a phenomenon such as intuition in this way may appear to run the risk of demystifying it by assuming that it can be understood. But understanding the fullness of the experience between two people in a counselling relationship could potentially add to the depth and meaningfulness of the whole enterprise. We might, for instance, find that 'intuition' was not an individualistic phenomenon, but a 'relational' one — that it was a function of the levels of communication and understanding achieved within the counselling relationship. We would no longer refer to 'the intuitive worker', but would be interested in the skills of the practitioner who could foster relationships in which intuition of therapeutic value was generated.

Who knows what the further exploration of client and counsellor experiences will yield. Counselling can be a vibrant experience carrying an intensity of relating which in itself is a major vehicle for therapeutic change. Perhaps further advances in our understanding of the potential of counselling can best be made by examining such experiences of the process. It is our view that the chapters in this book contribute to that understanding.

References

Adams, J., J. Hayes and B. Hopson (1976) *Transition: Understanding and Managing Personal Change*. London: Martin Robertson.

Axline, Virginia (1950) 'Play Therapy Experiences as Described by Child Participants', *Journal of Consulting Psychology*, 14: 53–63.

Blaine, Graham and Charles McArthur (1958) 'What Happened in Therapy as Seen by the Patient and his Psychiatrist', *Journal of Nervous and Mental Disease*, 127: 344–50.

Brannen, Julia and Jean Collard (1982) *Marriages in Trouble: The Process of Seeking Help*. London: Tavistock.

Caskey, Nicholas, Chris Barker and Robert Elliott (1984) 'Dual Perspectives: Clients' and Therapists' Perceptions of Therapist Responses', *British Journal of Clinical Psychology*, 23: 281–90.

Combs, A.W. (1989) *A Theory of Therapy*. Beverly Hills: Sage.

Crandall, Rick and Richard Allen (1982) 'The Organizational Context of Helping Relationships', pp. 431–52 in Thomas Wills (ed.), *Basic Processes in Helping Relationships*. New York: Academic Press.

Da Costa, M. (1985) *Frail Love Tokens*. Norwich: Edmund Norvic Printplan.

Davis, John, Robert Elliott, Marcia Davis, Mark Binns, Valerie Francis, James Kelman and Thomas Schröder (1987) 'Development of a Taxonomy of Therapist Difficulties: Initial Report', *British Journal of Medical Psychology*, 60: 109–19.

Dinnage, R. (1988) *One to One: Experiences of Psychotherapy*. London: Viking Penguin.

Dryden, Windy (ed.) (1984) *Individual Therapy in Britain*. London: Harper and Row.

Dryden, Windy (ed.) (1985) *Therapists' Dilemmas*. London: Harper and Row.

Elliot, Robert (1986) 'Interpersonal Process Recall (IPR) as a Psychotherapy Process Research Method', pp. 503–28 in Leslie Greenberg and William Pinsof (eds), *The Psychotherapeutic Process: A Research Handbook*. New York: Guilford Press.

Feifel, Herman and Janet Eells (1963) 'Patients and Therapists Assess the Same Psychotherapy', *Journal of Consulting Psychology*, 27(4): 310–8.

Fiedler, F.E. (1950) 'A Comparison of Therapeutic Relationships in Psychoanalytic, Non–Directive and Adlerian Therapy', *Journal of Consulting Psychology*, 14: 436–45.

Fitts, William (1965) *The Experience of Psychotherapy: What It's Like for Client and Therapist*. Princeton, New Jersey: Van Nostrand.

Gaunt, Stephanie (1985) *The First Interview in Marriage Guidance*. Rugby: National Marriage Guidance Council.

Greenberg, Leslie and William Pinsof (eds) (1986) *The Psychotherapeutic Process: A Research Handbook*. New York: Guilford Press.

Hobson, Robert (1985) *Forms of Feeling: The Heart of Psychotherapy*. London: Tavistock.

Hunt, Patricia (1985) *Clients' Responses to Marriage Counselling*. Rugby: The National Marriage Guidance Council.

Kagan, Norman, D. Krathwohl and R. Miller (1963) 'Stimulated Recall in Therapy Using Videotape — A Case Study', *Journal of Counseling Psychology*, 10: 237–43.

Kaschak, Ellyn (1978) 'Therapist and Client: Two Views of the Process and Outcome of Psychotherapy', *Professional Psychology*, 9: 271–7.

Klein, Marjorie, Philippa Mathieu-Coughlan and Donald Kiesler (1986) 'The Experiencing Scales', pp. 21–72 in Leslie Greenberg and William Pinsof (eds), *The Psychotherapeutic Process: A Research Handbook*. New York: Guilford Press.

Kolb, D.A. and R. Fry (1975) 'Towards an Applied Theory of Experiential Learning', pp. 51–86 in Cary Cooper (ed.), *Theories of Group Processes*. London: Wiley.

Kottler, Jeffrey (1986) *On Being a Therapist*. San Francisco: Jossey-Bass.

Kubler-Ross, E. (1969) *On Death and Dying*. New York: Macmillan.

Laing, R.D. (1960) *The Divided Self: An Existential Study in Sanity and Madness*. London: Tavistock.

Laing, R.D. (1961) *Self and Others*. London: Tavistock.

Laing, R.D., H. Phillipson and A. Lee (1966) *Interpersonal Perception: A Theory and a Method of Research*. New York: Springer.

Lietaer, Germain and Marleen Neirinck (1987) 'Non-Helping and Hindering Processes in Experiential Psychotherapy: A Content Analysis of Post-Session Comments', pp. 640–9 in W. Huber (ed.), *Progress in Psychotherapy Research*. Louvain-la-Neuve: Presses Universitaires de Louvain.

Lipkin, Stanley (1948) 'The Client Evaluates Nondirective Psychotherapy', *Journal of Consulting Psychology*, 12: 137–46.

Lipkin, Stanley (1954) 'Clients' Feelings and Attitudes in Relation to the Outcome of Client-Centered Therapy', *Psychological Monographs: General and Applied*, 68(1): Whole Number 372.

Llewelyn, Susan (1988) 'Psychological Therapy as Viewed by Clients and Therapists', *British Journal of Clinical Psychology*, 27: 223–37.

Llewelyn, Susan and William Hume (1979) 'The Patient's View of Therapy', *British Journal of Medical Psychology*, 52: 29–36.

Maluccio, Anthony (1979) *Learning from Clients: Interpersonal Helping as Viewed by Clients and Social Workers*. New York: The Free Press.

Markova, Ivana, C. Forbes and M. Inwood (1984) 'The Consumers' Views of Genetic Counseling of Hemophilia', *American Journal of Medical Genetics*, 17: 741–52.

Maslow, A.H. (1968) *Toward a Psychology of Being*. New York: Van Nostrand Reinhold (second edition).

Mayer, John and Noel Timms (1970) *The Client Speaks: Working-Class Impressions of Casework*. London: Routledge and Kegan Paul.

Mearns, D. and McLeod, J. (1984) 'A Person-Centered Approach to Research', pp. 370–89 in R.F. Levant and J.M. Shlien (eds), *Client-Centered Therapy and the Person-Centered Approach*. New York: Praeger.

Mearns, D. and Thorne, B. (1988) *Person-Centred Counselling in Action*. London: Sage.

Morrow–Bradley, Cheryl and Robert Elliott (1986) 'Utilization of Psychotherapy Research by Practicing Psychotherapists', *American Psychologist*, 41(2): 188–97.

Murphy, Philip, Duncan Cramer and Francis Lillie (1984) 'The Relationship between Curative Factors Perceived by Patients in Psychotherapy and Treatment Outcome: An Exploratory Study', *British Journal of Medical Psychology*, 57: 187–92.

Oldfield, Susan (1983) *The Counselling Relationship: A Study of the Client's Experience*. London: Routledge and Kegan Paul.

Orlinsky, David and Kenneth Howard (1977) 'The Therapist's Experience of Psychotherapy', pp. 566–89 in A. Gurman and A. Razin (eds), *Effective Psychotherapy: A Handbook of Research*. Oxford: Pergamon.

Orlinsky, David and Kenneth Howard (1986) 'The Psychological Interior of Psychotherapy: Explorations with Therapy Session Reports', pp. 477–501 in Leslie Greenberg and William Pinsof (eds), *The Psychotherapeutic Process: A Research Handbook*. New York: Guilford Press.

Parkes, C.M. (1972) *Bereavement: Studies of Grief in Adult Life*. London: Tavistock.

Raskin, N. (1974) 'Studies on Psychotherapeutic Orientation: Ideology in Practice', *American Academy of Psychotherapists Psychotherapy Research Monographs*. Orlando, Florida: American Academy of Psychotherapists.

Rennie, David (1984) 'Clients' Tape-Assisted Recall of Psychotherapy: A Qualitative Analysis'. Paper presented at the Canadian Psychological Association, Ottawa, 31 May.

Rennie, David (1985a) 'An Early Return from Interviews with Clients about their Therapy Interviews: The Functions of the Narrative'. Paper presented at the 34th Annual Meeting of the Ontario Psychological Association, Ottawa, 15 February.

Rennie, David (1985b) 'Client Deference in the Psychotherapy Relationship'. Paper presented at the 16th Annual Meeting of the Society for Psychotherapy Research, Evanston, Illinois, 19 June.

Rennie, David (1987) 'A Model of the Client's Experience of Psychotherapy'. Paper presented at the Sixth Annual International Human Science Conference, Ottawa, 31 May.

Rennie, David, Jeffrey Phillips and Georgia Quartaro (1988) 'Grounded Theory: A Promising Approach to Conceptualization in Psychology?', *Canadian Psychology*, 29: 1–12.

Rice, Laura and Leslie Greenberg (eds) (1984) *Patterns of Change: Intensive Analysis of Psychotherapy Process*. New York: Guilford Press.

Rogers, C. (1951) *Client-Centered Therapy: Its Current Practice, Implications and Theory*. Boston: Houghton Mifflin.

Rowan, J. (1989) *Personal Communication*.

Smith, M., G. Glass and T. Miller (1980) *The Benefits of Psychotherapy*. Baltimore: Johns Hopkins Press.

Stiles, William (1980) 'Measurement of the Impact of Psychotherapy Sessions', *Journal of Consulting and Clinical Psychology*, 48: 176–85.

Stiles, William and James Snow (1984) 'Dimensions of Psychotherapy Session Impact Across Sessions and Across Clients', *British Journal of Clinical Psychology*, 23: 59–63.

Strupp, Hans, Martin Wallach and Michael Wogan (1964) 'Psychotherapy Experience In Retrospect: Questionnaire Survey of Former Patients and their Therapists', *Psychological Monographs: General and Applied*, 78(11): Whole Number 588.

Strupp, Hans, Ronald Fox and Ken Lessler (1969) *Patients View their Psychotherapy*. Baltimore: Johns Hopkins Press.

Symington, Neville (1983) 'The Analyst's Act of Freedom as Agent of Therapeutic Change', *International Review of Psycho-Analysis*, 10: 283–91.

Timms, Noel and Annette Blampied (1985) *Intervention in Marriage: The Experience of Counsellors and their Clients*. University of Sheffield: Joint Unit for Social Services Research.

Valle, Ronald and Mark King (eds) (1978) *Existential-Phenomenological Alternatives for Psychology*. New York: Oxford University Press.

Wills, Thomas (1982) 'Nonspecific Factors in Helping Relationships', pp. 381–404 in Thomas Wills (ed.), *Basic Processes in Helping Relationships*. New York: Academic Press.

Yalom, Irvin (1966) 'A Study of Group Therapy Dropouts', *Archives of General Psychiatry*, 14: 393–414.

Zeigarnik, B. (1927) 'Das Behalten Erledigter und Unerledigter Handlungen', *Psychologische Forschung*, 9: 1–85.

Index

Index compiled by Peva Keane